JOURNEY TO SELF-AWARENESS

a spiritual notebook for everyday life

NOREEN MONROE GUZIE AND TAD GUZIE

PAULIST PRESS
New York/Mahwah

Book design by Nighthawk Design.

Library of Congress Cataloging-in-Publication Data

Guzie, Noreen Monroe.
    Journey to self-awareness : a spiritual notebook for everyday life
/ by Noreen Monroe Guzie and Tad Guzie.
    p. cm.
    ISBN 0-8091-3468-3 (paper)
    1. Spiritual life. 2. Conduct of life. I. Guzie, Tad.
  II. Title.
  BL624.G68   1994
  291.4—dc20   93-48995
                                       CIP
                                       AC

Published by Paulist Press
997 Macarthur Boulevard
Mahwah, New Jersey 07430

Printed and bound in the
United States of America

CONTENTS

In memory
of my mother
Gladys Monroe
who made
the ordinary
special

1

Introduction

Spirituality, like love and like power, is a word that escapes easy explanation. We all have a sense of an inner something that eludes boundaries. It's as hard to describe as being in love or feeling powerful.

You can identify moments in your life when you knew who you are and what your life is about. Behind those moments of special insight and self-awareness lies your whole experience of life, your life as you have lived it. These birthmarks and benchmarks are the foundation and the starting point of your spirituality.

Your experience is the only background you need to bring to this book. You might have a religion which is important to you, or you might not belong to any church or religion. This book respects religion but is not about religion. We write with the conviction that it is our everyday experiences which shape the spirituality of each person. The meaning of that elusive word "spirituality" will become clearer as we go along.

We offer you a framework for reflecting on your experience of life, on many important factors and forces, the main people and events and happenings that have shaped your spirituality. There are no doctrines or religious teachings in this book, no shoulds or oughts. Our intention is to invite you to become your own authority about your life and your spirituality.

you see
a thing
for the
first time
only once

Theodore White

We invite you to participate fully in the book, working with the questions for reflection that appear in each chapter. Use your journal or a coil-bound exercise book, a pad of plain paper and some colored markers. Or perhaps you do your most creative writing with a word processor. We have left space throughout the book for your personal jottings.

Put on some of your favorite music. Browse through family albums and boxes of snapshops, letters, old greeting cards, scrapbooks and souvenirs. Photos, home movies and family videos help us to revisit special moments in our lives. Looking through albums and other memorabilia reminds us of the people, the adventures, the misadventures, the celebrations, the settings of our stories. The old photo albums evoke times past, other days, how we grew up. We wonder how we have changed and how we have remained the same, and why.

Just as we invite you to participate in this book, so we have invited others to tell their stories. Hearing the stories of other people enlivens our fading memories and connects us to characters in our own story in new ways. The storytellers in this book are from many continents. They are between twenty-two and eighty-five years of age, representing diverse cultures and professions. We are grateful to our storytellers for their enlightening contributions.

We wrote many parts of this book in the village of Bibo, New Mexico. We wish to thank the Doughertys for making their restored adobe house available to us.

Denice Thibault designed the Celtic knots which you see throughout the book. The cover design and pages of calligraphy are Noreen's works of art.

2

Remembering

All week you have planned to work in the yard today. But now the sky is a forbidding grey. In annoyance you snap on the TV. As you change channels to find an encouraging weather report, an old movie title fills the screen and captures your attention. You remember seeing this film about one of your heroes years ago at the old neighborhood theater.

You turn up the volume. The theme music is familiar. You can't recall if the story was told in flashbacks or in chronological order. You find yourself watching the opening scenes to satisfy your curiosity.

Two hours and sixty-one commercials later, the story creeps to a conclusion. You wonder why you once found the movie so informative, inspiring, entertaining. Maybe your sentiments and priorities and values have changed so much that you are now bored by what once inspired you. Perhaps something got lost in the transition to the small screen. The movie was in technicolor, but everything seems black and white: the contrast between good and evil is blatant. The main character is flawless, decisive, too good to be true. Lacking dimension and depth, your hero comes across as a stereotype, a caricature, unreal.

Pouring yourself another cup of coffee, you fantasize about how your own story would be told. You begin reminiscing about your life. . . .

- What is the most courageous thing you have ever done?
- What is the most difficult thing you have ever done?
- What is the most extravagant thing you have ever done?
- What is the most selfish thing you have ever done?
- What is your greatest regret?
- What experiences have changed your life or set you on a new course of self-awareness?
- What animals or pets have played an important part in your life?
- What sports, entertainment, and pastimes have enriched your life?
- Are there particular cars, or airplanes, or boats or trains in your life?
- What towns have had an impact on your life, or have been the setting for significant moments? E.g. teaching in Appalachia, summer camp on a Minnesota lake, Vietnam in the '70s, jazz in New Orleans, May in London.
- What landscapes or terrains have had an effect on you? E.g. the seacoast, the Arizona desert, the inner city. How has that landscape affected you?

As you remember and reminisce, you wonder which film categories would best describe your life story: Adventure. Comedy. Romance. Drama. Documentary. Mystery. Musical. Horror. Western. Suspense. Action.

WE SEE THINGS NOT AS THEY ARE BUT AS WE ARE

H.M. TOMLINSON

jottings

3

Experience

Life is filled with profound moments, meaningful relationships, and peak experiences that are significant. We may not be aware of all the implications, but we know we have been affected.

A neighbor moves away, a co-worker is transferred to another city. You knew you had a few interests in common. But now suddenly the absence of this person makes you realize that the sharing was more than a relationship of convenience and casual conversation. The loss you experience astonishes you.

Our days are filled with routine activities, ordinary occurrences, casual encounters which we have forgotten about or laid aside or simply taken for granted. The word *experience*, as we are using it in these pages, involves more than a collection of happenings. Experience implies that you have been *attentive* to what has happened. You have reflected on the happening, and upon reflection you have discovered that the happening is in some way *significant* for you.

Daily routines like getting up in the morning and brushing your teeth, putting on your shoes, and plugging in the coffee pot probably have no meaning in your life. Maybe they never will. But if you are enduring a toothache, or a broken arm, or a power failure, you find yourself becoming attentive to insignificant routines that suddenly acquire significance.

Or take our experience of our own bodies. When we are young, our bodies are supple and they do what we ask them to do. When we are confronted with injury, or faced with illness and age, we are forced to recognize the significance of many bodily powers that we once took for granted.

Preoccupations, occupations, and everyday busy-ness often keep us from being attentive to what happens around us. If we are too involved to be attentive, we can't know what is significant in our lives.

Then there are the happenings which we ignore or repress. Misunderstanding and conflict are a normal part of any relationship. But alliances and partnerships break down, and friendships and marriages flounder when disagreements are not attended to, reflected upon, brought to significance, and assimilated into the relationship.

Some relationships appear to be harmonious but in reality are perpetuated by pretense or repression. In the case of alcoholism, substance abuse, sexual abuse, physical or mental battering, acknowledging our experiences begins the struggle of freeing ourselves from unhealthy bonds.

No one's life is free from problems, regrets, and disappointments. Too often the small joys and everyday pleasures are taken for granted, so that the ordinary paradoxes of life are experienced as hardships and injustices. The good things of life also need to be attended to and brought to consciousness and cherished.

When we are attentive to our experiences, we recognize how deeply we are affected by forces and situations outside ourselves, everything from the changing seasons to disruptive world events. When we are attentive to our experiences, we are able to recognize even the small beginnings and the quiet endings in our lives, and we appreciate the moments of renewal in between—the first blossoms of spring, the season's first game of golf, spring cleaning, the first swim of summer, the first vegetables from the garden, the first day of school, the first snowfall, and the first grandchild.

When we are attentive to our experiences, we become aware of the private milestones by which we measure ourselves. We become aware of poignant personal anniversaries that are not written on calendars or celebrated with cake and cards and candles.

There are many ways to be attentive to our experiences. No one method of reflection will suit everyone. We all have different temperaments, and so we reflect in different ways.

1. Some people seek a personal sacred space free from distraction in order to quiet down and meditate: a cabin in the woods, a restful room in the house, a chapel, a retreat lodge.

2. Some people ponder while engaging in their favorite activities and forms of relaxation: walking along a nature trail, listening to music, skating around an ice rink, sailing on the lake, rounding up cattle.

3. Some use what might be considered wasted time, like the time spent in waiting or commuting, as a worthwhile opportunity for thinking things through. Some people mull while performing mundane chores like vacuuming carpets or cutting the lawn.

4. Some write in diaries and journals. They prefer to reflect using the written word. Writing down thoughts and feelings helps many people to see more clearly the patterns and contradictions in their lives. Writing is a creative way to process the pain and relish the joys.

5. Some find that journal writing makes them self-conscious. They find themselves tending to write for some unknown other, or for an idealized self. Many people do their most authentic written reflection when writing to a

trusted friend. Vincent Van Gogh's letters to his brother Theo are a touching illustration of this trust.

6. Some people write for an unnamed audience. Often their desire is that sharing their experiences will assist others who are on a similar quest. For example, Sue Bender is an artist and family therapist whose fascination with the Amish lifestyle led her to a place of inner quiet and calm ritual which she recounts in *Plain and Simple: A Woman's Journey to the Amish*. Fritjof Capra is a physicist who, in *Uncommon Wisdom*, gives an account of the men and women who led him on his intellectual journey to new ways of thinking about science.

7. Some people have their own experiences clarified by being exposed to the experiences of people they have never met. Reflection on their own lives is stimulated by reading novels, poetry, philosophy, theology, biography. Drama and biographies on television and stage have been important means of self-discovery for many. Truckers who put in long hours on the road have benefited from books on cassette tape.

STORIES ARE NOT WINDOWS THAT TURN INTO MIRRORS. — SHEA

8. Some people find talking more enriching than writing. Conversations, light-hearted or intense, are one of their best ways to understand their experiences. They think things through better when they can talk things through.

9. Some who find oral expression to be their best way of reflecting on their experiences have no one to talk to. Or they do not want to take up other people's time with what seems like a selfish agenda. They use a tape recorder to keep track of their feelings, thoughts, impressions, and insights. Later they play back the tape, listen to themselves, record their clarifications. They need to talk to themselves before they can put anything in writing in a journal or personal workbook.

10. Some find that making art or making music is the best way to express their experiences.

What methods of reflection are most beneficial for you?

Reflection invites recollection. Recollection invites us to reenter and revisit our experiences. Revisiting our experiences enables us to reevaluate and re-vision our story, and thus to name our own myth.

As children we were told: "Learn from your experience— experience is the best teacher." Often the people who said this to us were horrified when what we learned from our experience contradicted *their* ideas of how life should be lived. But with time we come to trust our own experience, and one of the major truths it teaches is this: It is not what happens to us that is important; it is what we do with what happens.

- What has your experience taught you about youth?
- What has your experience taught you about aging?
- What has your experience taught you about responsibility?
- What has your experience taught you about nature?
- What has your experience taught you about intimacy?
- What has your experience taught you about religion?
- What has your experience taught you about death?

Here are some responses that people have given to these questions.

YOUTH AND AGING

"Youth has energy and enthusiasm and the will to make things happen when older people have given up or are too tired. The young don't fear to go where no one has trod."

"What youth lacks in wisdom is made up by resiliency."

"I am a young man who thinks that youth must be forgotten, betrayed and seduced before one is compelled into a new existence."

"Youth is something to get through as soon as possible. It is a time when mind and hormones collide, resulting in explosions that are often more damaging than beneficial. Youth is a time when one is burdened with adult responsibilities without the wisdom and the authority to manage those responsibilities. Humankind would probably evolve at a much more reasonable and accelerated pace if the youth years could be eliminated."

"At twenty-four I have some knowledge, some experience, some ambition, and some hope. Our inherited planet will treat us differently from previous generations because it has been abused for so long. I cannot help but feel apprehensive about our future."

"When you are young, there is always time to start over."

"In my head I am still the same person that I was when I first really identified myself at about age fifteen. I may have learned more since then, accomplished and dealt with more, but I can only wonder how that fifteen-year-old me did it."

"At the age of sixty-two, I feel younger than ever before. I am more conscious of life, the experience of it, the rapture of it, than ever before. I performed and achieved well, but now I can leave that to others to do. Now I can take time to do things I always wanted to do and never had a chance to do, like drawing, dancing, and cycling."

"When I was five I just wanted to be big. When I was ten I wanted to be fifteen. When I was fifteen I wanted to be sixteen. Now I would like to be forty-two again."

RESPONSIBILITY

"Responsibility is probably my raison d'être, my full-time occupation, something that each of us tries to avoid with varying degrees of failure. We seem to devote a lot of energy and talent trying to find a civilized way of avoiding our responsibility."

"Responsibility: I choose it."

"As I grow older I take more responsibility and am good and true to my word. I appreciate people who assume responsibility when they make a mistake."

NATURE

"Nature preceded man and it will succeed him. It is more complex and interconnected than we realize. It moves in finite cycles and we interrupt those cycles through our ignorance and at our peril."

"However much or little one enjoys nature as a youth, you can never get enough of it as you age. A relaxing ritual for me is looking out of my office window at nature in the marshland."

"Nature has always been a great nurturer for me. Surrounded by nature I become more fully alive and use my five senses."

"Hurricanes—what wrath! Earthquakes—what devastation! I'm in awe!"

"My father, a farmer, taught me to love the earth and to see nature's beauty. Nature has provided me with the scenario for most of my peak experiences."

"The first eighteen years bonded me to nature. Growing up on a farm with spacious fields, narrow brooks, meadows and woods cultivated my kinship with plants, animals, birds, fish. It drew me into a realm of mystery because I sensed an unexplainable energy in everything alive around me. As a child in Germany, I recall lying in the long grass facing the blue sky, playing a game with the racing cloud formations, then becoming still and wondering what is moving and shaping and making all of this. The cycle of birthing, blooming, fruiting, and dying instilled in me a sense of reverence and purpose for everything in nature. Wherever I am in the world, the magnificence of a brilliant sunset is always a sacred moment for me, and a long nature walk is still the most uplifting and refreshing experience for me."

INTIMACY

"Intimacy is a beautiful human experience. Intimacy has helped me grow in love, self-awareness and maturity."

"My experience has taught me the importance of a stable environment in childhood. I was raised in four different homes. Because of my lack of real intimacy as a child, I have problems being intimate now. I don't want to get hurt anymore."

"I treasure the intimacy of deep friendships."

"Intimacy is the joy of loving unconditionally."

RELIGION

"Religion is reassuring."

"Religion was something handed down to me from my parents. At first it seemed to be a lot of rules. It separated mind from body. Now I've grown to see the spirituality in it."

"Too many rules skew one's sense of self-reliance, and empty promises foster loss of faith. However, I cannot imagine growing up with no religion. I'm never short of idealistic naiveté, but I found it a major disappointment that the church too suffers from ill-used power, greed and selfishness."

"Religion is needed to explain and modify human behavior. As human beings began to violate the laws of nature, it was necessary to create myths and the laws that flow from myth in order to maintain our survival for as long as possible. We will one day move beyond our present understanding of religion, or we will perish."

DEATH

"When I went to the hospital for a total hip replacement, the patients in the ward I was in were all ninety years old. I was shocked when I saw the rough treatment they were getting. Aging frightens me, knowing this could happen to me."

"I only started to feel age after I turned eighty. The world seemed to be going so fast. All of a sudden new terms, new gadgets appeared and I am lost, not able to catch up. I feel so outdated."

"Being diagnosed with leukemia has made me sit up and take notice of time— it runs out. I've always lived down the road a piece, paying little heed to now. I've had to realize that *now* is all I have. I'm adjusting to the idea that *these* are the good old days!"

"My father's death when I was fifteen was the worst experience in my life, and for years the thought of death stirred only pain and loss in me. Later on, when I worked as a nurse among the Melanesian people of the Solomon Islands, I learned a totally different way of experiencing death. Sometimes I was called to distant villages to see very ill persons, and when I recommended that they

EX PER IEN CE · RITUAL · STORY · SYMBOL ·

NOREEN GUZIE

be brought down to the health center, they would refuse. They would accept some pain reliever but would insist on staying with their families. It dawned on me gradually how important it was for the dying to remain at home in their own place, among the family. Last words spoken by the dying were kept as sacred messages. Young and old would go up one by one to bid farewell, and all would remain and wail and mourn together until the burial. Everything stops in the village when someone dies—no cooking, no washing, no business. Grief and mourning take place right then and there. Life and death belong together, and the experience of death is really integrated into the experience of life. I sensed a great dignity about death when it happens this way."

"When I was a young boy I wondered if I would die. When I was middle-aged I wondered when I would die. Now that I am an old man I wonder how I will die."

Experience is multi-layered. It is especially through storytelling, symbol, and ritual that we uncover the various layers of our experience and bring to consciousness our personal myth.

The emblem depicts a cycle of story-symbol-ritual. In the next three chapters, we will look at how these three elements energize our experience.

jottings

4

Story

Before any of us had a story to tell, we were given names. That is a story in itself.

If your name is David Swing Hammer or Stephanie Bluebird, you are probably used to questions about your name. A story leaps out of your name, and people want to hear about it. Some of the people asking the questions have family names like Bridgeman and Brook, Washington and Jefferson, Taylor and Carpenter and just plain Smith. There are stories in each of these names too. But because of their familiarity these names no longer capture attention. Often surnames seem to be little more than labels, like the ones we wear on our lapels at workshops and conferences.

But names are never just labels. Our first names, middle names, last names all contain stories. Sometimes there is an intriguing story behind our names. Often the story is forgotten.

- Why were your given names chosen for you? What are the meanings of your names?
- Have you been pressured to live up to your name?
- Have you had to live down your name?
- How have you dealt with derogatory labels or nicknames?

- What descriptive phrase or title do you frequently depend on to describe yourself?

Titles and labels are a partial way of naming. They quickly provide social identification and give hints about our story. I am Doctor Gilmore's wife . . . I'm an alcoholic . . . I'm gay . . . I'm the President of Interfax Corporation . . . I am a survivor . . . I am born again . . . I am a battered wife . . . I am Reverend Rogers . . . I'm the non-achiever in the family . . . I am a separatist . . . I am a pro-lifer . . . I am a lifer . . .

Often when we use a label, we are letting people know how we want them to respond to us, and how we expect to be treated. Such naming can be a way of instantly informing, or gaining respect, or seeking attention. Some labels also offer an explanation, or solicit sympathy, or blame others.

Not every occasion is an appropriate occasion for storytelling. Therefore labels become necessary because they are an efficient way of naming and explaining one aspect of our story. However, labels and titles always define us too narrowly. They can create artificial boundaries for ourselves and others if we constantly rely on them because of our close identification with a profession, an institution, a movement, or a person.

> First
> with the names we are taught
>
> then
> with the names we choose
>
> we sing[1]

1. Michael Tarachow, *Somewhere Music, Somehow Song*, Fathom Press, 1981.

- Have you ever chosen a new name or added a name to celebrate a new beginning?

Recall a time when you needed to talk things through with someone and there was no one who could listen. Perhaps the other person was genuinely preoccupied and not able to hear you. Perhaps you told your story to someone you thought could hear and understand you, but you chose the wrong person or the wrong time. It was a waste of words, and disappointment was added to the difficulty. You felt that the story you told was quickly put in perspective with well-intentioned generic advice or tritely summed up with pious platitudes.

Experiences like this point to a basic truth about storytelling. If we can't tell our story, or if there is no one to receive it, we are left isolated and alienated. Henri Nouwen observed that "there is no hope for the future when the past remains unconfessed, unreceived, and misunderstood."

The spontaneous moments of confidence and understanding are often more fruitful than the planned conversation. Have you noticed that words sometimes flow more easily and we listen better when our hands are occupied and there is little eye contact? Bad news is broken, secrets are shared, healing laughs erupt as we paint a fence, wash dishes together, or drive along a country road.

Storytelling is one of the primary ways of *naming our experience*.

Your friend who moved out of town has returned for a visit, and the two of you get together for lunch. You haven't seen each other for three years. The storytelling begins. It's a natural way of locating ourselves and reconnecting with others. You both become animated as you tell your stories, and you know that the two of you have been able to pick up just where you left off three years ago. The friendship is everything you thought it was. This is a gift. Not all friendships survive time and distance.

You tell your friend about the difficult time you have been having with your elderly mother. You have told this story before. But you didn't tell it to your father the same way you are telling it to your friend right now. And you didn't tell it to your son in just this way either. You discover that you unconsciously edit portions of the story whenever you tell it.

Why do we keep improvising when we tell our stories? One reason is simple enough. Experience has many layers, and no single version of the story reveals all of the layers of any experience. The stories we tell are always an *interpretation* of our experience. When we continuously learn from our experience, we won't tell the same story in the same way twice, whether we are telling it to ourselves (for example, in journal writing) or to other people. We unconsciously omit some details and elaborate on others, sometimes to the point of exaggeration, so that the truth emerges.

"Twice-told tales are better than once-told tales, better as oral artifacts. They not only improve in structure and language by continual rehearsal; they deepen in meaning. Whatever it is you understand about a story told once, you understand a great deal more by hearing it again and again. . . . Some tales are more interesting than others, because they reflect how mysterious are the relationships we form as a family—accidents that give us our whole lives."[2]

The truth of a story includes much more than a correct account of facts and happenings.

Go to another city on a business trip or a holiday, buy the local newspaper, and read the factual report on the front page about the city council's opposition to the budget submitted by the mayor's office. You have some information, but nothing you could call truth. The word *truth* implies human meaning, relevance, significance, much more than facts. The editorial page in the

2. Roger Rosenblatt, in *Family Circle*, April 1, 1991, vol. 105, no. 5, p. 150.

paper might give you a lead if you want to understand the *truth*, not just the facts, of that town's experience.

Historians of folklore relate how romantic legends have been created out of common and mundane happenings. A young man, soon to be married, accidentally loses his footing and falls from a cliff. Within a generation, the rural community where the accident happened gradually gave birth to an elaborate legend involving evil spirits who, jealous of the young man's love for his beloved, drove him over the cliff. The event was remembered in a song sung by his lover, who laments his death and pledges her eternal and faithful love. Years later, while the heroine of the story was still alive, a folklorist drew the villagers' attention to the authentic historical details. "They replied that the old woman had forgotten, that her great grief had almost destroyed her mind. It was the myth that told the truth: the real story was already only a falsification. Besides, was not the myth truer by the fact that it made the real story yield a deeper and richer meaning, revealing a tragic destiny?"[3]

Storytelling gropes to tell the truth as we experience it. The cold hard facts don't make a story. This is why we inevitably edit and embellish. As we get older, the small family home becomes smaller and the large family home becomes a mansion. A casual parent becomes either callous or caring. The older we get, the colder the winters of our childhood become, the longer the walk to school, and the harder we worked for our weekly allowance.

- If you need to tell your story to someone, who is there for you? If there is no one to listen to you, what do you do?
- Whom are you there for?
- What are your favorite family anecdotes and stories? When were these stories told?

3. Mircea Eliade, *Cosmos and History*, Harper & Row, 1959, p. 46.

We live in the midst of larger stories than our own personal story. We grow up with the stories of our family, the communities that surround us, the town and time in which we were born, our nation, our religious tradition. Finally there is our cultural heritage, the largest story of all the stories that shape our lives—for example, the Judeo-Christian Greco-Roman heritage.

The six circles suggest the major stories that begin communicating values to us from the moment of our birth. These larger stories can also be called *myths*. Myths are stories that embody a community's experience, its values, its collective insights. The myths of Western culture are different from those of the East, just as the Christian myth is different from the myth of Islam or Hinduism. Owing to different myths, people's experience of life is very different— their experience of nature, the land, the passage of time and history, political structures, social relationships.

On a smaller scale, every community and every family has its own myth which has taken shape over the period of at least a generation or two. Different family or community myths will incarnate different attitudes about the values of work, money, education, and what is worthwhile in life.

All of the circles in the diagram overlap one another. This suggests how myths blend into one another as they go about impacting on our personal story. Perhaps you are the only child of college-educated parents, a Catholic born of Polish and German roots, a midwestern urban American whose youth was lived during the era of prosperity following World War II. The myths that molded your early story would be different if you are an Afro-American living in the South, the great grandchild of a slave.

And different if you are a Canadian of Scottish descent, the youngest of six children, raised on a farm in the western prairies by Presbyterian parents during the depression of the Thirties.

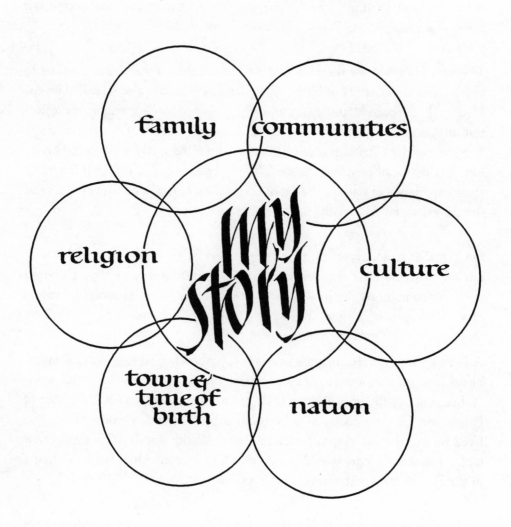

And different if you are a Pueblo Indian, the eldest of five, living on a reservation in New Mexico, raised by your maternal grandmother.

The myths of family and our nearest communities, the neighborhood, the church, perhaps the corner tavern or the country club, the enclave of people who share our parents' lifestyle—all of these larger stories nurture the formation and development of our personal story long before we know what a value is. Our personal story has already taken a distinctive shape long before we are even aware of making our own choices.

Not many of the choices we make in life are made on the grounds of reason and logic. A thorough process of discernment, a reflective process that weighs all the pro's and con's of a decision, is a luxury we can afford only at rare moments. The real world in which we make choices calls on us to be spontaneous, inventive, attentive and responsive to what the moment demands. In that moment, here and now, we are affected by the irrational influences of family programing and the old tapes that keep playing subtly in the back of our minds.

In the real world, few of our decisions are made on the basis of ethical principles that we have consciously reasoned through objectively. Most of our day-to-day choices come from the values and the prejudices that have been communicated to us from the stories, songs, jokes, and myths we have imbibed. Our everyday choices are also greatly influenced by the expectations of the many communities to which we belong. It is essential to be attentive to the many stories that have been part of our formation, and to the unconscious myths that are part of our personal story.

- As you were growing up, how were you affected by:
    the town in which you were born?
    world events taking place at the time?
    your religious tradition?
    your ethnic heritage?

> your place in the family?
> poverty or affluence?
> divorce, illness, or death?

- What communities, groups, or institutions have nurtured or affirmed you?
- What communities, groups, or institutions have confined or alienated you?

"In the world in which I grew up, more choices meant a better life. It was true for both my parents and my grandparents. I was brought up to believe that the more choices I had, the better. . . . Growing up in New York, my parents' message had been 'Be a star,' though these words were never said out loud. . . . Achieve, achieve, I heard, and along with the words came a clear picture of the right way to be."[4]

- What agenda, qualities, or values did your mother promote by word or deed? Your father? Your grandparents?
- What community, group, or institution were you brought up to avoid or fear?
- If you could ask each of your parents and each of your grandparents *three questions* about their stories, what would the questions be? The purpose of asking is to understand these persons better and to clarify portions of your own story.

Countless writers have argued that *individualism* is the main characteristic that distinguishes Western and North American culture from other world cultures. From the days of Benjamin Franklin and *Poor Richard's Almanack*, our society has valued getting ahead on one's own initiative. This means rising above the strictures of social class and caste, making a break from old myths and values, and forging one's own myth through wit, effort, and ingenuity.

4. Sue Bender, *Plain and Simple*, Harper, 1989, pp. 8–9.

Being an individual is certainly an important value in our society, but we are not by any means the *independent* individuals that our culture tends to enshrine. Reflecting on our personal stories is not a narcissistic exercise in which we attend only to ourselves. We cannot authentically attend to our own story unless we recognize our *connectedness* to others and to the larger stories that have helped to sculpture our own.

"Every psyche is a private theater filled with scenes and characters. Listen and you will hear your father, mother, brothers, sisters, children, lovers, friends, enemies, teachers, and heroes acting out their dramas on your stage. Hearing the multiple voices within yourself will remind you that you belong to a special clan. Your people still inhabit you."[5]

Personal integrity and self-esteem demand that we acknowledge those who have come before us, and that we understand the part they have played in the development of our personal myth. Knowing your grandparents' stories and their times helps you to appreciate your parents' stories, how in turn their personal myths have evolved, and how you have benefited and suffered as a result of these many layers of experience and larger stories.

The more we are able to learn about the people who have impacted on our story, the better we understand our own motivations. Why do we do what we do? Why do we respond the way we do? Why do we react the way we react? The support, encouragement and generosity of others have energized us to pursue our personal goals. On the other hand, the jibes or skepticism or scorn of others may have motivated us to prove ourselves.

- Who has harmed you by neglect, repression, or manipulation?
- Is there a person in your life whose sacrifice or goodness or gifts make you feel inadequate or indebted?
- Is there a person whose attentions and loyalty are a burden for you?

5. Sam Keen and Anne Valley-Fox, *Your Mythic Journey*, Tarcher, 1973 & 1989, p. 2.

- Whose name isn't mentioned anymore in your family story? Whose pictures are missing from the photo album? Is there someone whose absence from your story through denial or withdrawal causes you sorrow?

- Is there someone in your story whom you have chosen not to forgive?

Our memories are unconsciously selective. Sometimes we look to the past for what we need in order to validate the myth we currently have about ourselves. That's why it is never too late to have a happy childhood. And it's never too late to have an unhappy childhood, if that is what we are looking for to explain who we are to ourselves. As Ashleigh Brilliant remarks, "Some of the things that will live longest in my memory never really happened."[6]

Sometimes we get caught up in sentimental nostalgia or wistful remembering. "What's dangerous about nostalgia is that it's phony. It's a daydream in reverse. Like thinking we loved the books of our youth, when all we love is the thought of ourselves young, reading them."[7]

If we are at all flexible, our personal truth expands over time to include some things we once found false or contradictory. The villain of our youth becomes our midlife mentor, and the friend becomes an adversary. Were we blind to the mentor? Were we betrayed by the friend? Or have *our* priorities and allegiances changed?

The more we are able to *name*, the less inclined we are to *blame*. It is crucial to name and understand how we have been affected by the stories that have surrounded us. It is important to acknowledge the role we have played in the stories of others. The less we are inclined to name, the more likely we are to blame, to dismiss our failures or exaggerate our accomplishments. However, not everything can be analyzed or explained or named. We need to leave room in our life for surprise and for mystery.

6. Pot-Shots no. 722, Brilliant Enterprises, 1975.

7. Amanda Cross, *Poetic Justice*, Avon, 1970, p. 140.

time is a
dressmaker
specializing
in
alterations

Faith Baldwin

- What have been the significant benchmarks and milestones in your life?
- What have been the most important relationships in your life?
- Who have been your mentors, and how have they mentored you?
- How have you made a difference in other people's lives?

My life has been an experience of many facets and many mentors, and only now am I realizing the importance and value of the teachings with which I was prepared for life. My father died of leukemia when I was four years old. From the day that my mother stopped breast-feeding me, I was with my father every day. He took me everywhere with him. I was told that he'd talk to me constantly, even before I was able to speak. Some of his words live on through me in a subliminal way.

My paternal grandfather, a man of quiet dignity and much given to introspection, played a large role in my life after my father's death. Grandpa Frank Yellow Bird was a gardener, and he taught me a love and responsibility for the earth. We worked together in the camp-grounds near Pigeon Lake. I never knew him to eat at a table. He always ate on a place set for him on the floor. He told me, "What I am saying to you today may not have much meaning, but remember what I say. As the days pass, what you remember will bring forth the meaning of my words." Today I am still being taught by him.

I was in an Indian Residential School for part of my youth. There I met a kitchen worker who was the daughter of one of the patriarchs on the Ermineskin Reserve. She used to bring me extra fruit from the kitchen, and we became friends. We would go for long walks together. She was like the older sister I never had. "When you are older," she told me, "you will know many women. Some of those women may give you a gift they can give but once. How you receive that gift will have a bearing on how you are remembered. It is your responsibility whether you will be remembered in fondness or in anger."

Later in life I was adopted by Joe Roan, who has been the most instrumental in directing me to a good path. He was a traditional healer who taught me the rituals of the Lodgebuilder and the Firekeeper. I had to do four years in a hard place because of a stupid act, and before I left to do time Joe said to me, "You live your life as if you are still a boy! You were always treated special as a boy, but now you are still that boy. You get your own way, and it is a very selfish way to live. You already have children. Soon you will have grandchildren. When are you going to grow up and become serious about being a healer?"

I answered that I knew that a rage existed within me, and no one would be able to help me unless I did my own healing. If I cannot heal myself, how would I be able to heal others? If I undertook the power to heal, I would probably abuse it, just as I have abused many other things in my life. I would only be able to accept Joe Roan's gift when I was sure I would not abuse it.

I now live on the shores of Pigeon Lake. This is my home, the place I grew up, and it has taken me a long time to finally get here. It is comforting to be home with my family.

—Rik Yellow Bird (Kosowkwaniw)

I met my mentors in 1956 through the newspaper when I challenged in an article the American principle of equality for all. The Robinsons, who were total strangers, called me and apologized for the injustices I had suffered. They taught me how to love "others" other than your own family, which is totally unthinkable to a Japanese mind.

During the Christmas season of 1972 I lost my first and last mentor when Mrs. Robinson died. It was the most devastating experience I ever had. I wailed. For the first time I felt my own mortality. Then reality demanded, "How are you going to survive without anyone to turn to? You are all alone!" I was panic-stricken. I regressed—

disoriented—lost all my self-confidence. In the dying process, how-ever, I came to the cold realization that I am now my own mentor.

—Masako S.

Maturity implies accountability, and being accountable includes acknowledging that we are not alone. A spirituality of the here and now invites us to look at the essential role that community plays in our lives. This is the community of our family and friends or the global community—and all the groups, gatherings, and alliances in between.

Have you had the experience of gathering with like-minded people to work with camaraderie and zeal on a worthwhile project? In time, the task was completed and those involved went their separate ways, seeing one another occasionally in the supermarket or the subway. You were surprised and disappointed that the fellowship ended with the project.

Then there are the times when people who appear to have very little in common meet on a short-term basis to accomplish a task. To everyone's surprise, they find themselves continuing to meet regularly, project or no project. An association or an alliance has become a community. A bond has been formed which goes beyond the immediate task.

Most of us are familiar with a tension between the desire to be alone and the need to be with others, or the need to be alone and the desire to be with others. Frustration and disappointment are bound to be part of our experience when we fully participate in community. Disillusioned, we retreat, deciding to go it alone.

But not for long. We remember the blessed times when everything came together in an unpredictable way. These experiences encourage us to forgive, reconcile, trust, and hope once more. We discover and rediscover that community emerges when and where we least expect it—and often when we most need it.

"Sometimes our light goes out," said Albert Schweitzer, "but it is blown again into flame by an encounter with another human being. Each of us owes deepest thanks to those who have rekindled this inner light."

jottings

5

Symbol

We make symbols for the same reason we tell stories. We want to retain our experiences, remember them, hold them in our heads and in our hearts and sometimes even in our hands. Storytelling does this with words, but words are only one kind of symbol. In the next pages when we use the term *symbol*, we mean mostly non-verbal symbols, symbols that don't depend on words.

Symbols appeal to our minds and senses in a different way from words. Words are the best way we have to be precise, unambiguous, clear-cut, specific. Symbols offer the best way to draw us into experiences that defy this kind of definition. Symbols are a way to express experiences that need more than words.

Long before words and language were developed, people were creating non-verbal symbols. The native totem poles we see today are no longer primitive artifacts, but they illustrate some of our most primitive symbols. The totem is like a coat of arms, displaying birds and fish and animals. These creatures personify wisdom or strength or courage, or whatever qualities the family or clan most values.

The fertility of the bull, the mobility of the horse, and the freedom of the bird may not speak very loudly to people who are well mechanized and thoroughly urbanized. But as mechanized and urbanized as you may be, how do you react when you see a snake? This creature has always evoked the awesomeness of life's energies. Slithering serpents can be deadly, but the serpent is also a symbol of life and healing. Ever since ancient Greece the serpent has been the chosen symbol of the medical profession.

It is not surprising that the *animal world* provides our earliest symbols for what is most momentous and meaningful in life. This is the portion of the world closest to our own, and it took thousands of years before human consciousness clearly differentiated itself from the animal world. Many of the earliest human drawings depict figures that are half-human and half-animal. Today, mixed creatures like these appear more commonly in children's dreams than in galleries of art. But it is not only children who enjoy *The Littlest Mermaid* or that section of our newspapers where dogs dance, tigers tiptoe, and all animals talk: the comics.

Like animals, *trees* figure among our earliest symbols. Maybe this is because trees join us to the heavens with their branches reaching into the skies, and to the underworld with their roots penetrating deep into the earth . . . but trying to rationalize a symbol makes for dry reading. It is better to let the experience speak for itself: Who doesn't rejoice in the blossoming of trees in spring? Who isn't saddened when the golden leaves of autumn have fallen? Who is gladdened by the sight of charred trees after a forest fire?

The symbol that is most associated today with the Christian religion is the cross. For early Christians, however, the cross was a terrible instrument for delivering a slow and painful death. The cross did not become a major Christian symbol until centuries after crucifixion had been abandoned as a form of capital punishment. It was the *tree* that was central for early Christians. They saw the cross as a tree, and for them it was the Tree of the Cross that springs into life and bears the fruit of eternal life.

It is no accident that there is a Significant Tree in most of the early stories of creation. Did you ever lie under a tree telling stories? Did you ever carve your name in a tree? Was there a special tree that sheltered you? Was there a significant tree in your childhood, a venerable tree in your yard? Perhaps it was a tree whose sturdy branches held a swing, or a tree you especially liked to climb. How did you feel when years later you returned to the old neighborhood and discovered that your tree had been cut down? Your tree probably had nothing to do with the Knowledge of Good and Evil as it did for Adam and Eve—or did it?

Stones fascinate us from the time when we are children, when we collect the interesting and unusual ones from the back alley. Why are we attracted to stones? Walking along a shoreline, we find it hard to resist picking up stones and skipping them along the water's surface. Why are we attracted to stone walls, stone houses, tombstones, stone fireplaces, cobblestone streets, rock gardens? Perhaps we attach value to stones because they symbolize a reality so different from our own. Stones last, stones endure. Their permanence and their colors intrigue us throughout life.

In many early cultures it was a very large stone, a *mountain*, the largest stone in the community's experience, which was seen as the center of the universe. All of the gods lived atop that great stone which was Mount Olympus or Mount Athos. When Yahweh made an alliance with the Hebrews and delivered his commandments to Moses, it was atop the great stone which was Mount Sinai. The sermon that Jesus gave, summing up his ethics, was remembered by the writer Luke as a sermon delivered on the flat plains of Palestine. But the weight of Christian tradition remembers this speech, along with the writer Matthew, as the sermon on the *mountain*. Matthew's symbolism carried the day, because where could such an important message be delivered except atop a great stone?

Cities and parks all over the world feature statues and arches and monuments of *stone* which rise above the earth as monuments to leaders and wars and victories. The Vietnam Veterans Memorial in Washington D.C. is a different kind of stone. It is a gash sliced into the earth, not placed on top of the earth. This symbol remembers 58,183 men and women who died or who are missing in action. The names are engraved in the stone in the order in which they died. This slab of black rock celebrates no victory. It sits in stark contrast to the large white memorials in the area.

The Vietnam Memorial is the most visited monument in the United States. Eyes search for the name of a loved one, then hands reach out to touch that name. The wall is a place for remembering, a place for grieving, a place for storytelling, a place to say farewell, and a place to meet and connect spiritually. Thousands of people have left mementos, gifts, flowers, letters at the base of this stone wall.

On the tenth anniversary of the dedication of the wall, one veteran remarked that at first he saw the wall as an attempt to bury the reality of the war. He said he felt hurt and insulted. But over the years he has come to love the wall, which he now sees not as a memorial to the dead but as a living symbol of healing.

The stones that attract us in our adult years aren't found on beaches or in back alleys. That isn't because their material value is any different. Rubies and diamonds and emeralds are precious simply because we appreciate their rareness and beauty. Some stones have such value that people are willing to live for them and die for them.

We put our treasured stones in *boxes* in order to protect them and preserve them. The symbolic power of boxes may come from the fact that we begin our lives in the container or vessel which is our mother's womb. There are famous boxes like the Ark of the Covenant, and personally symbolic boxes like the caskets in which we place our loved ones.

We decorate our special boxes, beginning with the shoe box or cigar box where we first put our special treasures. We continue putting what we value in boxes, vaults, safety deposit boxes, jewelry boxes, trunks, and hope chests. Who doesn't enjoy receiving a gift given in a box? Why is it that a gift contained in a box is somehow more special? Even empty boxes have an allure all their own. Don't you hesitate to throw out an empty gift box?

Kids' forts and children's playhouses are big private boxes where special things are kept in still smaller boxes. Did you ever have a *tree* fort where you looked down on everyone and felt powerful? Why are we fascinated by houses built on hilltops? Why are we curious about who lives in the penthouse?

We have been using words to invite your reflection on the importance of symbols. We have evoked examples of symbols that need few if any words in order to communicate the power of some symbols which represent universal human yearnings and experiences.

Real symbols deliver their message without explanation or translation. You know that a symbol isn't working, or it isn't really a symbol, when someone gives you a "symbolic" gift and then has to explain in detail what it means to them and what it should mean to you.

But many symbols are attached to a story, and it is only if you know the story that you can understand the import of the symbol. This is true of all *personal* symbols. Unless you share the story, no one knows that the watch you are wearing once belonged to your father who gave it to you when you started your first job. The candlestick on your mantle looks very ordinary. A casual guest does not know it was the only thing saved after a fire that destroyed your grandmother's home.

We are comforted by the fire in the hearth and captivated by the flame of a candle. Tales are told and songs are sung around the campfire and around the candlelit table. Fire is heat and light, but part of the fascination is that fire is destructive. It is tamed one moment and out of control the next.

Water is also life-giving and death-dealing. It is a two-edged symbol. This is why water appears frequently in stories about transitions from death to life or from the old to the new. The Hebrews' passage through the waters of the Red Sea is the climax of the story of their escape from death in Egypt. In the Christian rite of baptism, the water does not mainly signify cleansing or purification but rather a turning point, a passage from an old way to a new way. The messages sent by our dreams convey the same symbolism. Water appears in people's dreams especially at times of crisis or transition, when there are important decisions to be made.

- What articles of clothing have been symbolic of different stages of your life? What articles of clothing make you feel good about yourself?
- Look around your home. Of all the possessions, souvenirs, keepsakes and mementos you have gathered, which are *symbols* for you?
- Are you wearing something now that has a special meaning for you? Do you wear something that unites you with another person or community?

"I have a crystal hanging from a golden string in my window. It reflects dancing rainbow sparkles throughout my room. This has become a symbol of my sexuality and my affective life."

A young man from Indonesia writes: "I wear a ring which my mother gave me, and a necklace from my sister, and a small cross for the necklace from my niece. These unite me with three generations in my family. All are gold, a symbol of their pure hearts given to me and mine to them."

A Chicago woman remembers the time when she was a small child, and her aunt invited the family for dinner. "My aunt served swiss steak. I was attracted to the meat not only because I was hungry, but because I was intrigued with the round bone in the meat on the platter. I asked my aunt if I could have it. I was grateful she consented, because this bone had limitless possibilities. In the end it became a key chain. I slipped a small link chain through its wide mouth, and from the chain I strung all my keys. I still have the keychain, and whenever I look at it I remember a child's spontaneous creativity with the most mundane of objects."

"Throughout my life I had always wanted a brother. I'm from a family of two sisters, a mom, a dad, and me. I met Doug when we were in a correctional institution. We thought a lot alike, we're the same age, and we had a lot in common. Doug and I became best friends. We never lost touch with each other during the year we were out. Then I came to this penitentiary. Doug arrived about two months later. We were both new to the federal prison system. We were told bullshit stories to scare us. Doug decided that he'd watch my back and I'd watch his. We would only trust each other. We made a strong team. We would never rat on or backstab each other, and we wouldn't do anything to jeopardize our brotherhood relationship. We promised each other that if one of us became sick or got put back in jail, we would take care of each other's family. Doug is somebody I can turn to for help or in times of sorrow. Before he left prison last year, we both had the same tattoo done on our right hands. The symbol we had tattooed means Brothers Forever, a bond that will never be broken. Trust, truth, love, friendship, everything you can think of is in the symbol we chose. If this bond is ever broken, I will cut the tattoo out of my body. Death is the only way that my brother and I will be separated. I couldn't have asked for a better brother. God did answer my prayer."

- What stones have you collected? What stones are symbolic for you?
- What mountains or large rocks are significant for you?
- What object was given away, lost, or taken from you, and your sense of loss surprised you? Why couldn't you replace it?

"The bowl of our sacred pipe is made from Grandfather rock, which symbolizes faith. The pipe stem is from straight-grained wood, symbolizing truth. The tobacco, which comes from the earth, symbolizes kindness."

we are shaped and fashioned by what we love

Goethe

"After my father's death I discovered that I could provide the original art work for the grave marker. With a few instructions from the memorial company, I designed our family name entwined with wheat, symbolic of his boyhood on a farm in Manitoba. Dad was always supportive of my artistic pursuits, and he delighted in my tales about the students in my classes. We shared many experiences and had a great many laughs. To have been able to create this lasting final gift was an uplifting experience which helped to relieve the sadness of my loss, and each time I see his gravestone I am reminded of our happy times together."

"When I was ten years old my mother and my brother took me on a picnic. I was on a weekend pass from the boys' home where I had to live. I was very emotionally attached to my mom and my brother, and I missed them a lot. So while we were on the picnic I collected three twigs of different sizes. Each twig represented one of us: my mother, my brother, myself. I brought the three twigs back to the boys' home and put them on my window sill. The next day the cleaning lady threw away my twig family. I got so mad and no one could understand why."

- How have you been affected by the devastating forces of water or fire?
- How have you been comforted by the healing effects of fire or water?
- Do you have a box or boxes that are special? What do you keep in these boxes?
- Rooms are large boxes. What room has been a haven for you?

> I have always enjoyed reading and being by myself, and our kitchen is the room that comes to mind. When I was about eleven or twelve, I was often given the responsibility of making sure the house was clean and tidy. This was quite a chore for me because if things weren't "just right," as perceived through the eyes of an alcoholic mother and whoever accompanied her home on any given night, there was a price to be paid. The work didn't bother me, but the reasons for my having to do it were a constant source of irritation.

I can still see the linoleum floor all bright and shining from my scrubbing and waxing it. The floor got warm from the heat of the wood stove, and the burning wood gave off comforting snaps. The odors of the fire and the waxed floor gave me a real sense of comfort and accomplishment.

The best part was when I finished up early enough to have the room to myself for a while. I would heat up a snack in the oven and get my books from my "secret place." I would set my snack on the floor along with a pillow, and I would lie on the warm polished floor and read. That was my time and place to ponder and dream the dreams that the books incited in me. I can recall feeling peaceful within myself. My life offers me very little in the way of happy thoughts. I find few memories worth keeping, with one exception—the world I lived in "my kitchen."

—Joseph B.

To my six-year-old self, nothing could be filled with more possibilities than an empty suitcase. My small light-weight blue suitcase was a First Communion gift from my grandparents. The suitcase was an invitation to imaginary and real adventures: Once you have a suitcase, can travel be far behind?

The suitcase is small now, but at that time it seemed to me like a steamer trunk. I could pack clothes for a month's trek to the source of the Nile in what now would only hold a sweater and a book. The suitcase could be a life raft and an emergency shelter on a deserted island if I were ever shipwrecked. Sometimes it made me a junior James Bond. I fired suitcase-to-air missiles, intercepting doodlebugs before they could blow up our local museum. Many lives were saved. In my real life the suitcase often carried my father's tools, making me a professional bike mechanic to my friends.

Being given a suitcase, like getting a driver's license, opens up vast possibilities. The suitcase meant I could run away from home in style.

Once, at the age of eight, when I was treated unjustly, I packed my favorite clothes, two peanut butter and honey sandwiches, and a snapshot of my mother—so I could remember who I was mad at. I remember setting up camp in the corner of someone's lawn about a block from my house. My blue suitcase was opened to construct the walls of my little refuge. The trip didn't last long. Imagining the adventure was more fun than actually doing it.

—David G.

Colors are symbolic. Color sets a tone and invites a spontaneous emotional reaction. We all have personal color preferences. But no matter what your preferences may be, there are certain colors that create a predictable atmosphere. Without a sound color speaks to us. It communicates, influencing our moods.

We expect people with red hair to be hot-tempered. We associate blue with baby boys and pink with baby girls. Why don't hockey players and football teams wear pink or mauve jerseys? What color is associated with magicians? Why is white the traditional color for brides? In the old western movies what color of hats were worn by the good guys and the bad guys? What is the color of the helmets worn by the United Nations peacekeeping troops? What is your reaction when you see your national colors on display?

Colors provide us with symbols to convey our state of mind. When we are angry we see red. When we are depressed we feel blue. In a black mood, we can be green with envy. A villain is black-hearted, and a coward is yellow. We have golden moments when we are tickled pink and see the world through rose-colored glasses. We paint the town red.

We associate symbolic colors with different feast days and holidays. Decorations, greeting cards, and novelty items reflect this color connection. In North America we associate the harvest colors of golden yellow and rust and brown with Thanksgiving, red and green with Christmas, black with Halloween, red with Valentine's Day, green with Saint Patrick's Day.

Color is our easiest and least expensive means of changing and enhancing ourselves and our surroundings, thus lifting our spirits. Let's look at some of the symbolic and mood associations of color. Some colors, depending on how and where they are used, suggest contradictory moods.

BLACK—mystery, magic, darkness, silence, space, void, emptiness, grief, death

WHITE—light, purity, joy, awe, glory, death

GREY—stillness, security, dreariness

BLUE is the most universally appealing color. There are many blue tones, each with its own impact.

LIGHT BLUE—peace, calm, tranquility

MEDIUM BLUE—depth, strength, thought

DEEP BLUE—authority, power, enveloping silence, cosmos, space

VIOLET—melancholy, nostalgia, reflection, sadness, soothing, seductive

PURPLE—mystery, pomp, royalty, weightiness

RED—action, aggression, excitement, vigor, birth

DEEP RED—courage, passion, warmth

PINK—placid, warmth without aggression

ORANGE—ambition, gregarious, stimulating, vibrant

YELLOW—cheerful, light, optimism, lunacy

GREEN—fertility, freshness, hope, promise of renewal, restful

BROWN—earthy, reliable, steady, sturdy, drab

BEIGE—serene, non-committal

What colors do you associate with the foliage and landscape of your youth? If you are from Newfoundland or the New England coast, the greys and blues of this area can be soothing for you. But the drabness of these colors are often depressing to someone from Alberta or Montana who is accustomed to the high blue sky of the prairies. Reds, rusts, and browns can seem severe to some; these same colors are reassuring to people from New Mexico and Arizona. The forests of British Columbia and Oregon are very different greens from the greens of the Louisiana bayous. The landscape, foliage and climate surrounding your childhood home influence your color preferences.

- What is your favorite color? What is your reaction when you meet someone for the first time who is wearing that color?

- What colors lift your spirits?

- What color do you dislike the most? What is your reaction when you meet someone for the first time who is wearing that color?

- Are there colors that you find disturbing or depressing because they are associated with an unhappy time in your life?

- Look around the room. What is your reaction to the colors that surround you?
- Look at the clothing you are wearing. Why are you wearing those colors? How do they make you feel?

"In my country, Japan, red and white are the colors of happiness, celebration, and congratulations. These colors are used for New Year's Day, birth and marriage."

"The eagle's place on the Plains Cree medicine wheel is to the east. His gift is vision, his color is red. The buffalo sits at the southern part of the medicine wheel. His gift is kindness, his color is yellow. The bear is on the western side, the place of introspection. His color is blue. The wolf sits on the northern side of the wheel. His gift is movement, his color is white."

"Garnet red is my favorite color. I look good in it, and I feel good too."

"My favorite color is blue. I'm always disposed to someone who is wearing blue when I first meet her. Any shade of blue will do."

"The color that is most significant for me is violet. My mother made all of my clothes when I was a child, including dresses and coats. Then, when I was six or seven years old, she bought me a new coat for Easter. It was the most beautiful violet color, and I was so thrilled because this was the first coat my mother had ever bought for me. I felt so special and valued, knowing that my mother had chosen this coat just for me. Since that time, violet has been the color that symbolizes great value, personal worth, and beauty. Not only is violet my preferred color, but lilac, the purple flower of spring, is my favorite scent."

Recall the aroma of pipe tobacco, the pungence of pine needles, the stink of stale gym shoes, the comforting balm of fresh baked bread, the clean waxy smell of new crayons, the fragrance of spring lilacs, the musty odor of damp basements, the scent of a loved one.

Get the whiff of an odor or fragrance, and you are instantly transported to another time, to past experiences. It is impossible to recall a *scent* accurately. We cannot remember and describe a scent the way we can remember a piece of music and hum the tune. But scents evoke memories more quickly and more poignantly than a sight or a sound, a picture or music. We associate certain scents with particular people, places and events.

We anoint ourselves with fragrance and our anxieties are calmed. A few drops of perfumed oil and the bath becomes a luxurious experience. The magic of scent can transform us and our surroundings. You wrap a scarf around your neck, and the lingering scent of a loved one embraces you. You walk down the street, the aroma of fresh-baked bread catches you, and immediately you are back in Grandma's kitchen or your first summer job at the local bakery. You are riding the bus, and you recognize the scent of your father's after-shave. Uncontrollably you are pulled back in time . . .

- What is your favorite scent? Why does that smell appeal to you?
- What scents recall festive times and absent friends?
- Is there a scent that reminds you of a misfortune or a mistake that deeply affected your life?
- What scents console you or lift your spirits? How and when do you use these scents?

TRUST YOUR
EXPERIENCE

CELEBRATE
YOUR STORY

TREASURE
YOUR SYMBOLS

NOREEN GUZIE

There are many stories we share in common, and therefore symbols we all can recognize. Everyone knows the symbols associated with Christmas and Halloween and with celebrations like birthdays, anniversaries, and weddings. But mere custom and tradition do not guarantee the *vitality* of a symbol. When they are not part of our personal stories, many symbols lose their power and simply become decorations.

Have you ever attended a Christmas party where the house glistened with festive prosperity, and all the tree ornaments and table centerpieces were color-coordinated? Everything was purchased especially for the occasion. Much time and care went into beautifying the home. But you had a sense that none of the ornaments on display had a story behind them. None of the decorations were invested with the power of the personal story of the people who lived there.

Have you ever been to a wedding that groaned under the weight of decorations, but there wasn't a symbol in sight? Beautiful decorations put us in the mood to be receptive to the symbols of the occasion. But decorations are not always symbols. At this particular wedding everything is rented: the church, the limos, the groom's tux and all of the wedding party's outfits. The flowers are silk, so they won't wilt. Photos are taken as the bride and groom kiss and attempt to cut the frosted styrofoam cake—only the top layer is edible.

Symbols that have lost their power are symptoms of a culture that has become de-spiritualized. Few of us would want to return to a primitive world where every tree and mountain and stream is animated by spirits or trolls or ghosts. But for all the benefits it has brought us, our technological culture has also conditioned us to see our surroundings merely as objects to be measured and manipulated, as forces to be subdued and harnessed and controlled. The result of this modern mentality is that nature, even when it is wild, appears somehow detached from us. We have difficulty recognizing the symbolic reality of the world we inhabit.

Donald Pelotte, who is the first native American to be appointed a bishop in the Roman Catholic Church, tells of a truth brought home to him on the day of his ordination:

> My ordination as a bishop took place outdoors, in Red Rock State Park in New Mexico. There were ten thousand native people who came, and the ceremonies included native dances by all of the tribes of the Southwest.
>
> We also had 55-mile-an-hour winds that day. A hundred bishops were in attendance, and there were miters blowing and flying all over the place. During the ceremony, as I was prostrated on a huge Navajo rug which the priests had given me, I thought I was going to fly away myself on this magic rug! For a lot of the Anglo people, this was terrible, all the wind and sun and sand. We were there for three hours, and some of the Anglos had to go to the hospital afterwards for severe sunburns. In my closing comments at the end of the ceremony I decided to say nothing more than "Let's go home, take a good shower, brush our teeth, and get the sand out of our hair."
>
> And then, afterwards, an elderly Navajo lady came up to me and said: "I hear that many were disturbed by all the wind and weather today. But for our people this was a sacred moment. You were being consecrated by the sacred elements."

The last chapter explained how we live in the midst of larger stories than our own personal story, and how we are deeply affected by those larger stories. A diagram illustrated how we grow up surrounded by

the stories of our family,
the local communities,

the town and time in which we were born,
our nation,
our religious tradition,
our cultural heritage.

These are the major stories, the predominant myths, which shape the formation of our personal stories. Each of these stories is filled with all kinds of
symbols, and so these stories are the source of the symbols we grow up with.

But the six stories named here hold true only in a general way. Individual
differences are vast. Not everyone grows up in a two-parent family surrounded
by an extended family and a supportive community. Nor should any of the six
major stories be idealized. For many people, maturity involves breaking free at
last from old family programing—or from oppressive community values—or
from a narrow-minded religion—or from a confining ethnic heritage that is
unable to cope with life in a pluralistic society.

For others the problem is just the opposite. We are reminded today on all sides
that many of us have no experience of roots. Our mobile society has given rise
to the so-called nuclear family, a unit of parents and children with no extended family nearby. Divorce has further divided the nuclear family into the
single-parent family. As a result, some of us have been isolated from a whole
variety of larger stories: familial, ethnic, religious, cultural.

What takes the place of these stories? Television provides one answer. The
value gap is filled by the lifestyles that are modeled in TV soaps and sitcoms,
by the understanding of human experience that is endorsed by talk shows, or
by the Myth of the Good Life promoted in advertising. Television is a major
source of values especially for people who are cut off from the larger stories of
family and community and neighborhood.

Your vocation or your career is very likely an additional story, another circle,
by the time you are a mature adult. What is the myth connected with your

profession, and what are its symbols? As life goes on, more circles are added to the diagram. As we distance ourselves from some myths and symbols, others come into being and impact upon our personal story.

My mother planted the tree when we moved into the only house my parents would own until Dad's death—the tree that witnessed the hellos and goodbyes of their everyday lives for so many years. The tree blossomed every three months in the heat of our garden in Guayaquil, Ecuador, and when it blossomed we decorated the whole house with its fragrant branches.

We children grew into yong adults and left home one by one. Each time we returned, the tree was still there, though its branches had begun to show the marks of time. I remember when my parents were building an addition to their house, the contractor said, "Well, Señor, that tree is in our way, we'll have to move it." Dad's answer came immediately: "If you remove that tree, you are removing me as well, so please find another way to bring in your building materials."

Did the tree hear this conversation? I do not know, but a week later it was filled with new buds, as if to say "Thank you, friend, you saved me." The seasons passed and even though the house went through lots of changes, there was always a way to leave that tree untouched.

A few years had passed since Pat McTeague and I had founded our school, Colegio Nuevo Mundo, in the extension that had been added to my parents' house. Soon the family house was not big enough to accommodate the growing community of people living there. A new school was built a good distance away, and we had a long, tiring drive to and from school each day. So, the idea of building a new house on the new school premises was brought to the attention of my parents.

Their choice was either to stay in the house which Dad had built in the years when he was young and energetic, or to live with us in an emerging community of women who had this crazy dream of starting a *nuevo mundo*, a "new world" in education.

Love, and the desire to contribute to the cause, carried the day. Dad and Mom agreed to go with us. But from the outset Dad declared that he would for sure take "his" tree along. We told him that given the age of the tree, it would probably not survive the move. "Where I go my tree goes," he said, and it was left at that.

As the new house was being built, Dad had to arrange the settlement of two mortgages that were held on the old house. I remember vividly that Thursday afternoon of the third week in October when he came into the house, tired but with a smile on his face, and a paper in his hand. He went to Mom and said, "The house is all yours now. We do not owe a penny. Now you can sell it."

What happened four days later startled us with surprise and pain. Dad died suddenly on Monday. Our emotions were overwhelming, to say the least. We put him to rest, aware that he, a good father, had showed us the way to die with dignity. Then my mother and my brothers and sisters-in-law and I got together to reminisce, and we laughed and we cried.

It was very significant for us that on the day of his death, the old tree was full of flowers. It was then that Mom said, "Wherever or whenever we move, I'll take the tree with me."

My brother, an environmentalist, gave us all the details on how the tree should be transplanted, what time of day, at what depth, and in which direction it should face. He said it was of the utmost importance that the tree should be planted exactly the way it was at the old house, and so we marked the tree for north, south and so forth.

We followed the instructions step by step. We got up at five in the morning so as not to transplant the tree while the sun was at its hottest. It took us two hours to do it. By then, sad to say, it had lost all of its flowers. We watered the tree, we talked to it, we waited . . . It never came back to life. A few days later the tree lost all of its green leaves. The bare, brown, gnarled branches were all that was left.

We did not take the tree down. I think it helped us all to realize that Dad's departure was final. Many times you could see Mom trying to hide her tears when she saw the old tree. Then one day she said, "Sonya, why don't we varnish it and hang nice plants from it?" So we did. It was the beginning of a healing process. It was okay to let go. Dad was the foundation of new life, new ways of appreciating life and death. And whenever we see trees of the same kind that are in full bloom, we think of him with warmth in our hearts.

—Sonya Rendón

jottings

6

Ritual

Storytelling *names* our experience. Ritual *frames* our experience. Ritual happens when we step back from our busy-ness and take time away from our history-making. Ritual helps us to locate ourselves.

"Each morning I get up half an hour before anyone else in the house," writes Dorothy, a junior high school teacher. "I sit with a cup of coffee in the dimness of the living room. Sometimes I mentally plan my day. Sometimes I think over the past day and what went right or wrong. Sometimes I pray. Sometimes I doze a little. I began this practice around the time I found out that my mother was dying of cancer, when I had a lot to sort out in my own mind. That was twenty years ago. Now, if I ever oversleep and miss this quiet time, I feel cheated all day. This is my personal time to get in touch with me."

Rituals are never merely habits or routines performed in the name of duty. Real rituals involve *awareness of ourselves*. Rituals are opportunities for taking time out to think about ourselves and to celebrate the little and the great things that happen around us. Traditions and customs, especially during times of turmoil, give us a sense of comfort and continuity.

A ritual can be something you do on your own, like Dorothy's morning time. Perhaps you get up each morning at dawn to run two miles. This ritual gives you quiet time alone, and you never tire of the glow of the sunrise. Or you end your day walking the dog around the neighborhood. On these evening strolls you experience a letting go of the day's cares and sometimes a sense of thanksgiving for the good things of life.

You attend a concert or a play. You draw, you make something useful or useless. You sing, you dance, you play at your favorite sport. Even when you are singing or dancing or playing alone, perhaps especially when you do such things alone, you experience yourself uniquely, and the experience is exhilarating and renewing.

"I try to take time for a personal ritual every day," writes Frans, a European in his sixties who works in Africa. "What ritual I do each day comes from the experience that has the most energy that day."

> My ritual for the day may be gathering wild flowers from the lake shore and putting them in my room to celebrate the colors and scents and scenes I experienced at the shore. Some days I write a letter or I make a drawing for a friend and colleague to celebrate the friendship. Although my mother is dead, on her birthday I mentally invite her to supper. I light a candle for her (for me!) to celebrate her birthday.

> My ritual may be holding and bringing to my ear the seashell that is in my room, to celebrate and to listen to my inner authority. It may be making a poster of all the joys I experienced that day, to celebrate the rapture of life.

> It may be a good hot bath with music, to "celebrate" my tiredness and the limitations of my body. It may be just relaxing, taking time for myself in my own sacred space, when I have been too hard on myself.

> It may be working on my scrapbook, really a collection of rituals, and it has a special place for me. Every week I fill two pages with clippings, pictures, drawings, in order to celebrate and store happy memories.

Many personal rituals are unplanned. These spontaneous rituals celebrate a completion, a beginning, an accomplishment, a transition, a resolution. We need personal rituals as a way of celebrating and even validating our experiences.

You get your hair cut in a new style to celebrate a new era in your life. To celebrate an achievement you commission a piece of jewelry, or you buy a special book. Upon completion of a project you buy a plant or add a new place setting to your silverware. Or you spoil yourself with a new piece of equipment for your hobby. You add new fish to your aquarium. You listen to a favorite piece of music and eat a solo supper with candles and a good wine.

We associate articles of clothing with different rituals. Our closets hold vestments for the more solemn events and celebrations: the extravagant gown, the pressed uniform, the tailored suit. We have clothing for our private rituals as well: the threadbare jacket, the elegant red shoes, the faded bathrobe, the splendid silk shirt. Dressing for the occasion is a ritual in itself, whether it be the bride dressing for the wedding or the player suiting up for the game.

"When I know the meeting is going to be either tense or a time-waster, I put on the special tie. This tie has become a kind of vestment for me. Just putting it on in preparation for the meeting calms me down and changes my attitude."

• What symbolic acts or rituals do you rely on to mark important moments in your story?

• Do you have a personal ritual that you rely on to center yourself when you are lonely, or anxious, or overwhelmed, or confused, or depressed?

Celebration requires that we have something to celebrate. Family traditions and communal rituals give us a sense of belonging to something larger than this moment and these people. Traditions connect us to the past and to the future, giving us continuity and community. The ritual of decorating the

The
movement
into
the future
continues
to accelerate
mercilessly

James Zullo

Christmas tree portrays a sense of history and hope. Each year we retrieve the battered box from the basement or attic and open it with a sense of renewal. We carefully unwrap the ornaments from past years. Some of the newer ones are handmade, gifts from friends. The older decorations of wood and glass show the patina of age. We lovingly remember the people and good times and the stories associated with these decorations.

Most rituals involve other people than just ourselves. A child's earliest experience of ritual is a family meal shared around a table. Along with sporting events, the *meal* is a ritual that is common to every culture. Every culture recognizes the deeply human and spiritual significance of sharing a meal together. The Jewish tradition has a beautiful and remarkable genius for celebrating all that is important in life with a blessing at an ordinary family meal.

It is especially at times of ritual that storytelling takes place. In many families, events and experiences of the day are told around the dinner table. In many cultures and religions, special meals celebrate special events, and it is at a meal that the story is told and remembered. The stories recorded in holy books like the Bible were first told when people gathered for celebrations. If it were not for times of ritual, many of the world's most treasured stories would not have been remembered. Today as well, when people gather for a picnic, for a party, for a potluck supper, a meal is shared and stories are told and remembered.

Media portrayal of family life has changed over the years. In the movies of the '30s and '40s and '50s, most families were seen having breakfast at the beginning of the day in a sunny kitchen with ruffled curtains. They ended the day with an evening meal around a table in a well-appointed dining room complete with linen napkins. Covers of the *Saturday Evening Post* regularly featured Norman Rockwell families joyfully and harmoniously sharing food together—a bounteous Thanksgiving dinner, or a petite grandma with her freckled grandson at the local ice-cream parlor.

Family rituals have come on hard times in recent decades. How many times in the last twenty years have you seen a magazine cover featuring a family or a group of friends sharing a meal together?

But no family celebration is perfect. Norman Rockwell's paintings are charming idealizations. They aren't realistic depictions of family life the way most of us experience it. In every real family there are painful memories of difficult times that don't usually show up in photographs. There are old sibling differences, real or imagined. Negotiating around two family members who are at odds with each other is sometimes part of the tradition every time the family gathers.

Some people regress into teenage behavior when they return to the parental home to celebrate. Away from the family, they handle complicated social situations with ease. Away from the family and on the job, they are confident and rarely consult or seek a second opinion. But in the presence of parents they desperately seek compliments and affirmation. Reunited with siblings, some revert to the behavior of five-year-olds, becoming picky or competitive in a renewed effort to fight old battles.

How do family members welcome new members into the family? How do the sisters relate to the new sister-in-law? A widowed grandfather remarries. How is his wife received? The eldest son brings home his life companion. What is the family's response?

What happens when the only time we gather as an extended family is at Christmas, major anniversaries, or funerals? What happens when we gather without any effective continuity in the family's story, or without a real desire to participate fully? Agatha Christie's dapper detective Hercule Poirot gives a good explanation:

> Families who have been separated throughout the year assemble once more together. Now under these conditions, my friend, you must

admit that there will occur a great amount of strain. People who do not feel amiable are putting great pressure on themselves to appear amiable! There is at Christmas time a great deal of honorable hypocrisy. . . .

I am pointing out to you that under these conditions—mental strain, physical malaise—it is highly probable that dislikes that were before merely mild, and disagreements that were trivial, might suddenly assume a more serious character. The result of pretending to be a more amiable, a more forgiving, a more high-minded person than one really is, has sooner or later the effect of causing one to behave as a more disagreeable, a more ruthless and an altogether more unpleasant person than is actually the case.[1]

Reconciliation does not come automatically with a celebration. When there has been a rupture in a relationship, some chronic peacemakers use festivity as a replacement for a healing process that needs to begin elsewhere. The result is a time of tension, or at least frustration for everyone gathered. A festive gathering is not the time to attempt major changes in relationships or lifestyles.

"I used to do this all the time," said one aging matriarch. "I prided myself on pouring oil on troubled waters. Matters usually became worse instead of better. In my old age I came to realize that at a time of celebration, oil on troubled waters just results in pollution."

• Make a list of your family traditions. What stories and symbols are associated with these traditions?

• What are your most memorable family gatherings? Why are these events significant for you?

• How have these gatherings strengthened or altered your relationship with those present?

1. Agatha Christie, A *Holiday for Murder*, Bantam, 1962, p. 48.

- What rituals do you and a loved one have to celebrate your relationship?
- What religious rituals have been a spiritual experience for you?
- What civic celebrations or sporting events have been a renewing experience for you?

Some of our most spontaneous and authentic rituals take place outside the family circle, where camaraderie encourages storytelling and celebration. "Dave and I often mark our victories by stopping at a little neighborhood pub," writes Lorna, who lives near Boston. "Our pub is like Cheers on TV, where 'everybody knows your name and they're really glad you came.' Our town is made up of Irish and Old Yankee New Englanders who are averse to knocking on one another's doors. But they will readily socialize, celebrate, or commiserate with one another at the pub."

Consider the ritual surrounding sports. The stories and the statistics, the uniforms, the abundant symbols and flamboyant rituals surrounding sporting events are for many people major ways of celebrating seasons and the passage of time. Few religions in our time can assemble such enthusiastic, emotional, and committed followers as can the liturgy of sports. Many fans celebrate the rituals of sports alone, at home in front of the TV set, wearing the team colors and toasting the players with souvenir mugs. Sports are communal events, but they can also be significant private rituals.

Television has created customs. Many families gather once a week to watch a favorite TV show. They make popcorn and share quality time together. They look forward to this timeout from a hectic week.

Religions provide us with rituals and symbols for celebrating feast days, high holidays, and rites of passage. As people move away from organized religion, they frequently turn to civic groups and sporting events to provide seasonal celebrations that mark the passage of time. Many organizations and companies hold festive gatherings to acknowledge corporate and personal anniversaries. If you don't celebrate within a religious community, if you don't work for a company with special traditions, if your family doesn't live nearby—with whom do you celebrate and mark the passage of time?

Good ritual calls for responsibility, whether it is a birthday party or a golden wedding anniversary. We need to take time to deliberately plan with whom and how and when and where we will gather to celebrate. Otherwise we will become observers of ritualistic activities rather than participants in ritual. As years go by, circumstances change. Many old forms don't fit anymore; we need to be flexible and innovative. Some of us are timid about creating our own customs and innovating ritual, so we keep repeating the unexamined customs of childhood. Or we lead a life without ritual where one day is the same as the next. Commemoration, celebration, ritual and festivity connect us to humankind and are essential to the human spirit.

This past Christmas was our second Christmas without any of our parents. Our two young boys no longer have grandparents to visit, so it was important to begin new traditions to fill the emptiness. Christmas Day is a time of quiet celebration, going to church, opening gifts, phoning long distance to relatives and friends.

My husband's sisters and their families now travel to join us on Boxing Day. So we spend the remainder of Christmas Day in preparation for their visit. After our Christmas dinner the table is cleared, and out comes the wrapping paper for making party hats and poster board and glitter for the place cards. We make personalized Christmas crackers containing miniature novelties, carefully chosen by the boys for each guest, and slips of paper with jokes and riddles selected in the morning as we read through corny joke books together. The bustle of scissor-passing, tape-tearing and ribbon-tying draws us together in anticipation of the delight of others.

—Beth M.

- Are there any rituals or symbols which you have adopted or inherited from others that need reassessment or revitalizing?

- At the present time is there a ritual you regularly participate in which is disruptive to your life?

- Are there any stories, symbols, or rituals you have neglected or abandoned which need retrieving?

- Is there something in your life that needs celebrating or commemorating with a ritual?

Ritual embraces tears as well as laughter. *Mourning* is a ritual act which enables us to absorb a death experience so that we can go on with life. This includes not only physical death, but also the death of a relationship, the loss of a job, or a separation caused by a career move. It includes the death of an idea or a cause that once motivated us but now has fulfilled its purpose, and we feel a loss.

We grieve when our idealized personal heroes and heroines fail and fall. We grieve over other losses: the loss of our own ideals, the loss of freedoms we took for granted, the loss of physical or financial independence, even our loss of memory.

North American society expects us to recover quickly from any kind of death experience. In a culture that values efficiency, grief is supposed to have an expiry date. Grief shouldn't show too much and it shouldn't last too long, annoying our friends or affecting our job performance.

Have you ever had the experience of not being able to get on with things because you weren't able to grieve? You weren't able to mourn. You weren't able to share your pain. You weren't able to express your disillusionment.

WE SHALL NOT CEASE
FROM OUR EXPLORATIONS.
AND THE END OF ALL OUR
EXPLORING WILL BE TO
ARRIVE WHERE WE STARTED.
AND TO KNOW THE PLACE
FOR THE FIRST TIME.

T.S. ELIOT

Sometimes a good cry is just the ritual act that is needed to make our sorrow conscious. Tears are often needed to bring closure to a portion of one's story so that life can continue. We need rituals for acknowledging difficult passages, painful transitions, and losses in our story.

Throughout his years as a parent of twelve children, our father taught us much about how to live and, in five short weeks, about how to die.

When he received the final diagnosis, he and our mother called their children and families together. We met in the garden of the hospital grounds, standing around in a loose circle. Dad had brought a roll of toilet paper from his hospital room. He tore off big pieces and slowly gave them out to each one. He gave us all permission to cry and said he too was having a hard time with this news. In the following weeks, he set aside time for private conversations, for affirmations and reconciliations, and for speaking about his most important learnings, values and memories.

During his illness he was able to be away from the hospital several times. On Sunday of the Thanksgiving weekend, neighbors and friends from the church community generously prepared a Thanksgiving feast for our family and aunts and uncles who had come from far away. Many family members went with him to church and then returned home to share this last feast with him.

He spoke strongly and lovingly about gathering around the family table to share meals. Dad talked about how he and our mother began the practice of holding hands around the table to bless the food. This became a simple and powerful way for them to connect with all of their children, if only for a moment. Sometimes holding hands at mealtimes was the only and the best contact our parents could have with us as we moved through the difficult years of adolescence. Returning home as adults with our friends or spouses or children, we knew the circle could always be expanded to welcome us home. After the funeral service, we went to the funeral home where his body was to be cremated. We stood in a circle around the coffin, held hands and said our last good-byes as a family.

This kind of touch was very important to him during his illness. Dad spoke of how he received strength whenever someone held his hands, or massaged his feet. In his last few days he spoke of giving this strength to my mother, to his children and grandchildren, and to the sick man in the next room.

Perhaps it was his gift of strength that enabled us to work together to prepare our public farewell. My father had made two specific requests for the funeral service. One was for a favorite scripture reading of his which tells of a feast where all are welcome. The other request was that his sons and sons-in-law carry his body down the aisle at the beginning of the church service. The rest he left to us.

I liken our experiences to the days when families used to prepare the body for burial, build the coffin, and dig the grave. Our large extended family gathered, his twelve children along with spouses and aunts and uncles, some around the big round table in the dining room, others around two computers in a room upstairs. Being urbanized adults of the late twentieth century, we "built" the words of the obituary, the funeral services, and a booklet of readings, poems and prayers important to our father and our family. Those who knew how to use the computer typed and edited. Others would come in and offer suggestions and encouragement. Several times we did a print-out of the work up to that stage and circulated it to those sitting around the table, ensuring that everyone had a chance to comment, add or delete.

I experienced these preparations as a fascinating blending of spiritualities. In choosing readings, prayers, music, poems and reflections, we all had to grapple with our beliefs, traditions, memories and our different ways of expressing them. When one of our aunts suggested that we begin the prayer service by saying the rosary, some of us younger ones were startled. This traditional Catholic practice was just not part of our own experience. She told a story about how our grand-mother daily prayed the rosary for each of her seven children as she went about her work. So we decided we would begin in this way, linking ourselves to our father's mother and to her faith.

One brother suggested a scripture reading which describes struggle and resolution within a father-son relationship. Though this seemed to be an unusual choice for a memorial prayer service, we agreed. It reflected our brother's experience and that of other family members as well.

Our father died during the season of autumn. He had been able to spend a lot of time outside in a wheelchair during the warm, golden fall days. He died early in the morning just as the first snow fell. We decided to offer crocus bulbs to those who came to mourn his death and celebrate his life with us. The bulbs symbolized for us the mystery of life and death, holding within themselves the promise of new life throughout the cold winter.

Five years later, my crocuses are still blooming. I look forward to seeing them poke their blossoms through the mulch of dead leaves, and to the memories of my father which they evoke.

—Kathleen Quinn

jottings

7

Ordinary Time

Celebration is a pause for taking time out from our history-making. The stories, the symbols and the rituals of celebration carry the essence of who we are as individuals, as a family, as a community. Not all celebrations are spontaneous emotional highs. Some are harmonious gatherings preceded by hours of planning, preparation, and moments of anxiety. Some are stifling events that are an occasion of tension rather than accord.

Regardless of what kind of experience it is, celebration returns us to everyday life with new eyes and a renewed sense of who we are, and sometimes with a new sense of purpose. We re-enter Ordinary Time enlightened and energized.

For all of us, Ordinary Time is taken up with many activities that we find either tedious or stimulating. Time drags by, or we are running out of time. Einstein once explained his Theory of Relativity in this way: If you spend two hours talking to an attractive woman, it seems like minutes. If you sit on a hot stove for a minute, it seems like two hours.

Here are some activities that are easily overlooked when we ask ourselves "Where did the time go?"

For some, the morning shower is a routine that is essential for waking up. For others it is a relaxing ritual, a time alone to prepare for the day. The evening bath may be necessary to wash away the day's grime. Or it can be a time for soaking in the day's experiences.

- What portion of your day do you spend on personal appearance and grooming? What part of your body do you spend most time thinking about?

For some, cooking is a chore. For others it is a creative activity. For some, food is simply nourishment. For others food is gift, an occasion to socialize, or the focal point of celebration.

- How much time do you spend thinking about food, preparing food, and eating and drinking?

Shopping is a necessity. For some, going to the store is something to be put off as long as possible, and you get someone else to do it if you can. For others, wandering around a mall is a way to relax. Shopping is entertainment.

- How much time each week do you spend shopping? Is there an item which you will never have enough of and which you always enjoy shopping for?

There is a difference between cutting the grass and grooming the lawn, just as there is a difference between housework and homemaking.

- How much time do you spend beautifying and caring for your home and its surroundings? Is caring for your home a chore, a hobby, or a luxury?

Resentments and regrets can rob us of time and energy. Fretting over past hurts and lamenting our mistakes prevents us from living in the present moment. Frequently we brood over a particular person or revive an incident with the same result, namely, bitterness or hopelessness. We are drawn to replay the unfortunate scene over and over again.

- How much time do you spend fighting old demons?
- Are there any lingering resentments or misunderstandings from your childhood years that trap you in the past?
- Whose presence in your story causes you anxiety or stress, taking up your time and draining your energy?

We take sleep for granted, not appreciating its restorative power until we have a night of lying awake when sleep eludes us. The next day we feel fatigued, fragmented and unfocused. Some think sleep is a waste of time and put it off as long as possible in the name of productivity or duty. For others, their bed is a nest or a womb, and sleep is a refuge or an escape.

- How much time do you spend sleeping? How much time do you spend resting, relaxing, reflecting and daydreaming?

We wait in lines at the bank, the post office, the cafeteria, the toll gate, the stop lights. Often we wait for the mail, we wait for the right job, we wait for someone else to make a decision. We wait for a child to be born. We wait for the right moment, the right person.

- How do you pass the time while you are waiting?
- What is your definition of a "good time"?
- What routine chores and activities do you look forward to doing because they offer you moments of reverie and contemplation?
- Make a list of the people you most enjoy spending time with.
- By the time we get what we want, we often don't want it anymore. Or we don't know what to do with it. What did you plan for carefully or strive hard to achieve, only to be disappointed? What did you work for that wasn't worth the time and effort?
- Is there a person, place, thing, or activity you feel bound to because of your investment of time or money?
- What offends you more: wasting money or wasting time?

"Eternity isn't some later time," said Joseph Campbell. "Eternity isn't even a long time. Eternity has nothing to do with time. Eternity is that dimension of here and now that all thinking in temporal terms cuts off. And if you don't get it here, you won't get it anywhere. The experience of eternity right here and now is the function of life."[1]

A spirituality of the here and now invites us to look at the role of work in our lives. The first question we are often asked when we are introduced to someone is "What do you do?" or "Where do you work?" Have you ever had the feeling that the conversation became stilted when you couldn't provide a satisfactory response?

For some, work is a four-letter word. It is something to be avoided unless it guarantees power or financial gain. Others struggle to find work. Many wrestle with ways to find meaning in work.

We can experience work as a chore and a distraction that keeps us from more worthwhile endeavors. Our associates are tolerated as part of the job. Spirituality, creativity, and relationships are experienced and cultivated in our off hours.

On the other hand, some of us are dedicated to duty or immersed in our profession to the point of devotion. Following schedules, keeping score, achieving and pursuing consume our waking hours and define our spirituality. We lose ourselves in our work; we have no off hours.

A story that looms large for all of us is financial concern. The symbol that is most prominent in this story is money. Money is in fact a *spiritual* invention, one of the first great symbolic products of the human mind. It was a wonderfully ingenious way to get around moving your harvest physically to the market and trading it for the physical goods you needed. Money freed us from

1. Joseph Campbell *The Power of Myth*, Doubleday, 1988, p. 67.

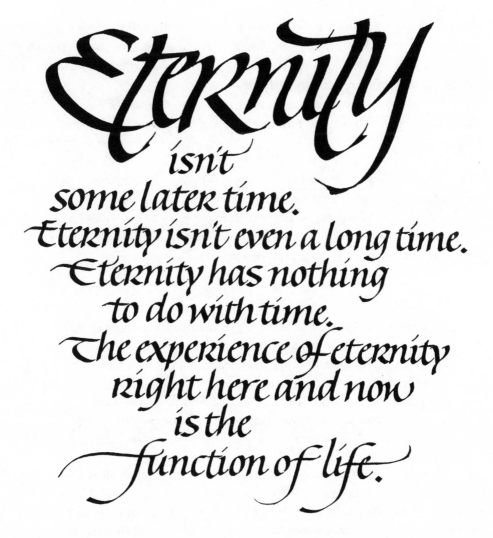

Eternity
isn't
some later time.
Eternity isn't even a long time.
Eternity has nothing
to do with time.
The experience of eternity
right here and now
is the
function of life.

Joseph Campbell

many physical burdens so that we could give our time and energy and spirit to other endeavors.

Our communities benefit from monetary contributions and from constructive economic growth. But greed is like fire or water that has gone out of control, because it seems to deal only death. Acquiring money as an end in itself is one of the most destructive substitutes for more spirit.

Many have been able to find fulfillment in the work they do. Here are some examples:

> I work in the graphic arts industry. My job involves camera work, color stripping, and plate making. What I do is both challenging and interesting because every job is different. It is gratifying to see a job run off on the presses and turn out exactly the way you intended it to. I consider myself very lucky to have a job I really enjoy.
>
> —Gene Thibault

> My satisfaction in being a nurse who works with mentally-ill adults comes from within myself. Because of society's attitude toward the stigma of mental illness, as well as the lack of socialization of many of the patients, there are not the usual outward displays of gratitude that one sees in other parts of the hospital, such as flowers and thank-you cards. One must develop, with very little feedback from the patient, a sense of what is helpful in the therapeutic relationship and what is not.

> What I have learned most in working with the mentally ill is about myself. Every meaningful encounter with a patient has caused me to receive as much as I have been able to give. I have learned to understand the process of a feeling such as anger, rather than hearing only content. I have learned to examine the judgmental feelings coming from my own background which cause me to experience the patient in a certain way. It would be dangerous for me to say that I do not have any further feelings that need to be dealt with because, to me, this

would mean that I have no further potential for growth. It would also mean that I am not experiencing the patient as an individual. Working with others who have problems has taught me a humility about what I bring to the encounters. I can only offer to others as much as I have, and for me this implies a responsibility to co-evolve with the patient.

—Irene Ens

I have taken time off from college. I work at a day-care with children between the ages of two and five years. I like the freedom of supervising the children on my own and being a participant in their games and creative activities. I enjoy the boys' and girls' conversations and the interesting questions they ask. They have different mental and physical capabilities, and it is fascinating to see how they solve problems, settle arguments, and deal with new situations. I am rewarded by the children's affection and the fun of observing them in action. To some kids I'm a big brother, to some I'm a father figure, and to others I'm a friend.

—Michael G.

As a calligrapher I study, practice, and design different styles of writing. There is an endless variety of letterforms, and each one in its own way enhances the written message. When I design menus, certificates, or titles, I enjoy the interaction of working with clients, helping them to discover the possibilities of hand lettering.

I also like to combine written letters with painting, collage and printmaking to create unique artworks, including books. It delights me when written text, abstract images, and a painterly play of light and shadow all work together to make a many-layered message for the viewer. Of course, not all such attempts are successful: the journey from concept to creation is fraught with pitfalls and blind alleys. Therefore, I make a special effort to enjoy and learn from the process itself rather than focusing on artwork as a finished product. The time spent thinking about the work is usually much greater than the time spent actually doing it.

—Lindley McDougall

I am a chartered financial consultant, and I own the business with my husband and another associate. My specialties are retirement planning and disability insurance. I love the independence of my work—I answer only to my clients. Each day is different, each client is unique, and my opportunities for personal and financial growth are unlimited. I like building long-term relationships that turn customers into clients and friends. I know my work prevents people from becoming poor.

—Leslie Macdonald Francis

Working with wood has brought me great satisfaction. I have been a journeyman carpenter for sixteen years and have worked on many projects: warehouses, apartment blocks, houses, furniture, inlaid boxes for friends, and children's toys for family members. I have been a drug and alcohol counselor, and my motive was that I was a child of an alcoholic parent and I wanted to do my bit. But unlike carpentry, you don't see the end result. So I left my counseling position to take up hammer, saw and nails.

A truck-driving job came to me from an uncle who owns semis and needed help. This slaked my thirst for wanderlust. But the gratification at the end of a run was nowhere as great as the gratification I felt when I would help a family move into one of the houses I had built.

An assistant hotel manager's job came to me after I had renovated a hotel. The owner liked me and my work so much that he trained me for the job. The money was good, but working around drunks was more than I could handle. I returned once again to woodworking. The challenge of drawing plans, ordering materials, dealing with exacting measurements, cutting and assembling the project, and the ever-elusive zero waste of materials—this is all a challenge I find energizing and fulfilling. My woodworking has given me my greatest joys. The perks, other than being my own boss, are the opportunities I give myself to pursue my hobbies, do landscaping, travel, and search for the so far evasive Ms. Right.

—Walter S.

How do *you* spend your Ordinary Time?

Make a chart following this example.

ACTIVITY	MOTIVATION, REASON FOR	REACTION
walking the dog	exercise for both of us	7
weekly meetings with Jack	he insists it's necessary	2
weekend shopping at farmer's market	get fresh produce, enjoyable drive and relaxing time in the country, family time together	9

In Column 1, make a list of the *activities you are involved in.* These are the activities related to your relationships and your inner life; and the activities related to your vocation, occupation, or profession. Remember to include projects, meetings, gatherings, educational pursuits, hobbies, sports, physical exercise, recreation, and your contributed services or volunteer work.

In Column 2, alongside each of the activities in Column 1, write a *word or phrase* that gives the *motivation or reason why* you engage in this activity.

In Column 3, *rate your reaction to each activity* on a scale of 1 to 9. A rating of 1 indicates that the activity is frustrating, annoying, draining. A rating of 9 indicates that the activity is enjoyable, energizing, affirming.

Read over what you have written down. Are there some activities you consider a waste of time? Is there anything that is noticeable by its *absence* from the list? Perhaps there are things you want to do and have put off doing.

Among the different dimensions of your life—emotional, social, intellectual, physical, intuitive, spiritual—what dimension do you give the most time to? What aspect gets the least attention?

We have many ways of marking time—season to season, visit to visit, payday to payday, from one annual vacation to the next. Cultures and religions have many different ways of dividing time and marking important events. There are days of rest, days to fast, days to feast. Like the seasons, these cycles of celebration give a rhythm to time that enlivens our days and balances our lives.

- What special ways do you have for dividing and marking Ordinary Time?
- Do you ever declare a personal holiday and simply take time off? Is there a pattern to these unofficial holidays and spiritual sabbaticals? How do you spend your time on these days?
- If you could have more of something, what would you want more of?

jottings

8

More Spirit

There came a moment in time when the human spirit was born. We don't know when it happened for the first time. When it did happen, whenever the spark was lit, we began the long trek toward what we know as human consciousness—the *spirit* you bring to this book as you read these pages.

Historically, this didn't have to do simply with the ability to make tools. A chimpanzee can figure out how to use a stick to knock down a bunch of bananas from a tree, and a beaver knows how to build a dam. *Spirit* is a word that says something distinctively human.

The invention of the plow some twelve thousand years ago was a work of *spirit* in this sense. The plow was a simple tool, enabling us to grow a surplus of food. But the spiritual innovation here was a revolutionary leap. Today we deliberately plan for tomorrow. We have savings and pension plans, we buy insurance, we make plans for the future. It all began with the plow. The invention of the plow meant that the human spirit had expanded to include consciousness of *tomorrow*—a time which does not exist except in our minds, in the human spirit.

The invention of language, somewhere around the time of the plow, was another great spiritual breakthrough. Language gave us the only means we have, then or now, to hold the future in our minds and to think and talk about the future as though it were before our eyes. Language soon brought about the invention of writing, another great spiritual creation.

But it was not until around 600 B.C., near the beginning of the great flowering of culture in Greece, that we find writings which contain not just reports about what people did or what they experienced, but *reflections* on what they experienced.

In the West, Greek culture brought the beginnings of science and philosophy, ways to understand both the universe outside ourselves and the world within ourselves. Our debt to ancient Greece is well known. What is often overlooked is the astonishing landmark in the evolution of the human spirit which took place at this time—that is, the ability to reflect on our experience, to be conscious of our selves, to be *self-aware*. Over the centuries this self-awareness has resulted in all of the artistic, literary, and scientific products that are encompassed by the word "civilization."

Now here we are, at the end of the twentieth century. What sort of self-awareness is yet in store for us?

The human story seems from the beginning to involve a drive, a desire, a quest for ever more spirit. We have never been able to tell in advance what "more spirit" will be. But this much seems constant throughout human history: Whatever spirit we have, it's never enough. Our loftiest images of a heaven, of a life that transcends this life, revolve around higher consciousness, more love, more life, more spirit . . . the images keep expanding, and the only constant is the word *more*. That word is perhaps the best we can do when we try to guess at the future of the human spirit.

Spirituality, as we use the word in these pages, is a name for this quest for *more spirit*. It is a word for our yearning to connect with something, someone, beyond ourselves. The history of spirituality is in part the story of the many millennia it took for humankind to reach self-awareness. Today, whenever we are operating at the highest level of spirituality which humanity has attained, we are using our wondrous ability to be *self-aware*. The questions for reflection throughout this book have sought to engage your own self-awareness.

Religious writers have often said that love is the highest act of the human spirit. But one cannot truly love unless one is self-aware. Reflecting on our experience and giving ourselves over to the task of becoming self-aware is the foundation for love. It is also the foundation of a mature spirituality.

The quest for more spirit came before religion, but religion has accompanied this quest since the dawn of the human spirit. From the most ancient of times religion has provided stories, symbols, and rituals to name and interpret human experience. Religion has collected and codified and handed on spiritual traditions of profound value. No religion ever fully embodies the spiritual energy of a person or of a people. But over the centuries, religion has given countless people a way to enter more fully into the experience of life.

Until recent times, religion was the only institution in Western culture which was committed to a spiritual interpretation of life. In the climate of a scientific culture which has tended to scoff at anything which isn't measurable or quantifiable, religion has held open the door on the Unknown. In the past few centuries, if a person became interested in *spirituality*, it was usually because of a newly found interest in *religion*, and this was usually accompanied by a conversion to formalized religious practices.

But these days, being a "spiritual" person is no longer synonymous with being a "religious" person.

College students today who would not consider taking a course with the word *religion* in the title are keenly interested in the topic of inner growth. *Spirituality* names something they want to learn about. Great numbers of people today enroll in yoga classes and journaling workshops. Many have been awakened to a spiritual life through seminars and retreats offered in business and professional circles which promote personal wholeness. The idea of a "spiritual" dimension in life and in nature is becoming accepted by sciences like psychology and physics, which would have spurned the idea a century ago.

Religion, in other words, is no longer the only mediator of spirituality and of the quest for more spirit.

- Psychologist Carl Jung found in his work that people are unable to get on with their lives unless they can name the goal for which they are striving. How would you describe the goal toward which you are striving?
- What insight has been a turning point in your life?
- What in your life seemed to be settled, and now is calling for attention?
- Can you recall any recurrent dreams that have nagged at you for attention? Can you recall any major dreams which you know had something important to do with the course of your life?
- What three things do you most believe in?

Imagine that you are standing on a shoreline. It is a blustery day. The surf rushes forward and pounds against the sand. Further along, barriers have been driven into the shore to hold back the water and protect the land. The sound of the crashing waves excites you. You are soaked by the spray as you stand at this boundary of sea and land.

This experience is a metaphor for the way we sometimes experience life itself—as opposing forces in conflict with one another.

"Spiritual" life is often understood as something that conflicts with ordinary life, "secular" life. The world of the spirit is elevated; it is other and apart from the everyday experience of pleasure and pain. Our bodies belong to this lower world which is less spiritual. Our souls on the other hand belong to a higher world. Being a spiritual person therefore means rescuing the soul from the

WHAT
FAITH
CONSCIOUSLY
SEEKS
LIFE
INEXORABLY
REVEALS

DICK WESTLEY

impulses of the body and avoiding the dangerous temptations of a materialistic world.

These are some of the basic elements of a form of spirituality which is well known to anyone who is reading these pages. This view of life, with its conflict between body and spirit, its split between nature and the supernatural, is usually accompanied by many other dualisms —God vs. Satan, grace vs. sin, sacred vs. secular, good vs. evil, right vs. wrong. This spirituality often includes a good many shadow projections in order to explain the darker side of life. Evil is always everywhere and always Other: in some other person, in some other creed or race or color, in the World or the Flesh or the Devil— never really in Me or the things I hold dear.

Few people would see themselves on the extreme end of this spectrum, where the nasty things in life are always someone else's fault. But most of us have to admit that we are affected by this way of thinking. When something goes terribly wrong and we ourselves have done everything right, we are tempted to look for someone to blame.

Nations and cultures also have a spirituality. In the early '90s the nations of the West look with astonishment at the downfall of the Soviet Union. That collapse poses an appalling challenge to our politics—and to our collective spirituality. Our governments have been managed by a generation of people who have seen the world in terms of the dualism between capitalism and communism. We now have to deal with the *absence* of that great Opposite which was Soviet Communism. Are there leaders in our midst who have the vision to guide our countries and economies into the future without having to arouse us with the threat of some new Satan? What is the new story that will replace the old story, the Cold War story which shaped our foreign policies for more than a generation? Will the new story, like the old one, be based on a conflict of opposites? These are questions involving the bottom-line spirituality of nations.

Spiritualities characterized by *struggle* have been popular throughout the ages. This is true for individuals as well as for nations. Many people are energized by competition and combats. Their personal stories center around meeting challenges and overcoming obstacles. They thrive on defending the truth and fighting for what is right. For many it is natural to see the spiritual life in the same way —as a struggle between forces inside and outside ourselves.

- What is the driving force in your life at this time?
- At this time of life, between what two conflicting realities do you feel poised?
- What ideals have you had to let go of as you have faced reality?
- What do you fear most?
- What do you look forward to?

Experiencing the shoreline as a boundary between the powerful forces of sea and land is real and important. It is crucial if you are an architect who is designing condominiums to be built on the beach, or if you are an engineer whose task is to prevent erosion of the coastline.

But this is not the only way to see the shoreline. There is another way to see the world where there aren't the boundaries which our minds project into the world. Let's take another look and experience the shoreline in a different way.

You are walking along the shore. It is your favorite time of the year. You experience how the land joins the water and how the water embraces the land with its ebb and flow. The water and the earth come together into a unity which is magnificent to behold. Water and land are not separate; there is only continuity, and everything is one. What you experience and what you take in is the oneness, the wholeness of the tremendous display of nature which is altogether embracing. There are no boundaries here. Even the boundary of your body disappears into the wholeness of it all, and you experience your own self as part of the All of things.

This experience is a metaphor for the change of consciousness which is taking place all around us. The quest for *more spirit* has been leading us in new directions. Ken Wilber describes this change as a move toward "unity consciousness" and away from "boundary consciousness" with all of its dualisms and conflicts and warring opposites.[1] Unity consciousness is not new to mystics, who have always valued a holistic way of seeing life and living it. But the kind of consciousness once nurtured by only a few has now begun to change our culture as a whole. This change is a profound spiritual change, and it is affecting the spirituality of millions of reflective people.

Changes of this magnitude are usually reflected in intellectual and social movements which at first appear to be fads. Today's ecology movement is perhaps the most widely known expression of a shift toward unity consciousness. This movement involves a transformation of some four hundred years of Western thinking which has seen nature as something to be conquered and controlled. Now, suddenly, an entire culture is learning that nature is not an adversary. Ecology is no longer a fad. It is a *spiritual* movement in the fullest sense, one which calls for profound changes in the way we act, not just the way we think.

"At a certain stage of the movement, people began to realize that in order to be serious environmentalists, it was not good enough to belong to the Sierra Club and to pay your dues if you did not also try to separate your garbage, turn off the lights, and practice voluntary simplicity. There has been a whole evolution of consciousness in the environmental movement. The people on the leading edge of the movement are now those who embrace right living and voluntary simplicity. Narrowing the distance between what you say and what you do has almost become the *sine qua non* of the environmental movement. It is becoming a moral imperative that once you begin to make all these connections, you can no longer speak with forked tongues. You can no longer

1. Ken Wilber, *No Boundaries: Eastern and Western Approaches to Personal Growth*, Shambhala, 1985

hope

IS DEFINITELY NOT
THE SAME THING AS
OPTIMISM. IT IS NOT THE CONVICTION
THAT SOMETHING WILL TURN OUT
WELL-BUT THE CERTAINTY THAT
SOMETHING MAKES SENSE-
REGARDLESS OF HOW IT
TURNS OUT.

Written in prison by Vaclav Havel
who became President of Czechoslovakia

go around describing what everybody should do without being a model yourself. So you end up not pointing the way but being the way, and if you can't be
the way, you just have to get out of the ballgame because you become such a
charlatan."[2]

The feminist movement is another expression of our quest for more spirit and
of the move toward unity consciousness. Feminism would best be spoken of as
a new *humanism*, because this movement affects the spirituality of women and
men alike. We are discovering the dark side of patriarchal ways of understanding and running the world. We are learning about the neglect and suppression
of the feminine principle which belongs to all of us, men as well as women.

There is impressive evidence showing that some cultures in the ancient world
reveal no sign of male domination, no weapons, none of the technology of
warfare. There was a time, long before the appearance of patriarchal religions,
when *partnership* between men and women was the model for living.[3] Today,
as society struggles with the issues of justice and equality between men and
women, we are striving to create a new partnership—or to restore a very
ancient one. The issue here is not only social and political. It is a spiritual
issue which affects everyone's answer to the question "Who am I?"

- How does your lifestyle reflect your concern for nature and the condition
  of the earth?
- How does your lifestyle reflect your concern for social justice and human
  rights?
- What is the role of literature, drama, the arts, or music in your life?

  During the Depression years of the early '30s, my parents were the
  proud owners of a grand piano. My older sister learned to play the

2. Hazel Henderson, in Fritjof Capra, *Uncommon Wisdom: Conversations with Remarkable
People*, Bantam, 1988, p. 281.

3. Riane Eisler, *The Chalice and the Blade*, Harper & Row, 1987.

piano by ear (music teachers were unheard of in our part of Saskatch-ewan). Many hours and years of patient practice made Sis a talented musician. Not to be outdone, I would prop myself up on the piano bench and through dogged determination I, too, learned to play our beloved instrument. When I was ten or eleven years old, I progressed to accompanying Sis with my $5.98 guitar.

I remember one cold winter night vividly. Farm chores were completed, there was a cozy fire in our pot-bellied stove, and Father was seated in his favorite rocker, reading his Swedish newspaper. Mother was busy sewing and mending clothes for our growing family of five. Sis and I spontane-ously decided to play every song we could remember, including even some verses of the latest songs on the Hit Parade which we had memo-rized from listening to radio broadcasts through earphones.

We had played over a hundred songs when we decided to play our version of "Over the Waves." This piece was originally written for the accordion and was played often on Scandinavian programs of that era. While Sis and I were playing, Father quietly went into his den and opened his steamer trunk, which we never dared open ourselves. This trunk contained his most personal and precious belongings. He took from this special box his piano accordion, which had been secretly stowed away all these years, unknown to us! He came into the room proudly playing "Over the Waves" along with us. The stunned look on my sister's face soon turned to tears of joy, while dramatic me just fled the room with excitement! Oh, if only the videocamera had been invented back then!

When we had finally calmed down, we asked Father why he had never told us that he had a piano accordion, let alone that he was such an excellent musician. A look of deep caring came over his face as he explained that he wanted us to develop our own style of music, and he did not want to interfere with our formative years of musical growth.

Today I play my "oldies" on my trusty keyboard at many senior citizens' functions in Calgary, Alberta, and my early childhood memories recharge me for yet another stellar performance. Music has enriched my life. It gives me a means of self-expression and a sense of accomplishment. Music sustains me when I am feeling down, lonely, or confused.

—Leonard C.

I am an artist. Thinking about my introduction to art, I first smell cow shit, then turpentine, then Juicy Fruit gum. It is a hot summer afternoon. The wind stirs a stand of trees, remote and to the left. The clouds breathe all the shapes my imagination can bear, all the forms absent from the prairie I am lying on.

Her breathing also comes in gusts as she negotiates each gesture. My mother is perched on the edge of an aluminum lawn chair, with her squinted eyes too near the propped up canvas to see the barn she is painting, and the painting she is painting. The ruined barn, collapsing into the earth, looks healthier in paint but just as impossible.

She always made something exceptional out of the ordinary. Her brush strokes, lean and drawn out, suddenly snap up and away like the tail of a signature. Luminous, viscous colors eked from the tiniest metal tubes are thinned with turp and muted by a reverse alchemy into the somber tones of the scene: an economical and self-conscious Van Gogh. Flat-knifed white shocks the surface, yet mysteriously fades into the distant oily clouds. I once tried to imagine that the magic of the paintings evaporated just because I saw all the steps in the process.

It is now thirty, and twenty-five, and seventeen years later. There is nothing I can see that is not also made of paint.

—D. Garneau

The world of science overwhelms most of us. We appreciate the benefits that science brings, and we happily or not so happily leave it to others to understand the experiments and theories that make the benefits possible. There is also the dark and frightening side to science which we prefer not to dwell on at all. The bottom line for science seems to be *making things*. The result has been both great boons and great bombs.

So it is a surprise for many people to learn that science has recently been making important contributions to spirituality. Science too is becoming part of the movement toward unity consciousness, and has been changing its mind about what the world looks like. As many scientists now see it, there is no way to understand even the most minute particle of an atom unless you understand the entire system to which it belongs. Scientists are now using metaphors like *network*, the *web*, the *mosaic*.

This is a very different way of seeing the world. From the earliest years of schooling, most of us have been taught to take a thing apart and analyze it, break it down into its smallest pieces in order to understand it. The new approach, in every field from physics to health care, is to put things *together*. Until we see the interconnectedness of things, whether in biology or in business, we have not understood what is most essential.

Tony Dimalanta, a psychiatrist, describes how this way of seeing things affects his work: "In psychiatry there is tremendous pressure to be a missionary—that is, to save everybody but to forget about yourself. That is one of the reasons why the suicide rate is so high among psychiatrists. What happens is that the patients transfer their problems to the psychiatrist, and if psychiatrists cannot take care of themselves they reach the point where they become desperate and commit suicide. Therefore, when I do family therapy, I make the family understand that part of my role is to take care not only of the family, but also of myself. If I have needs, I make them understand that this is part of the whole system we are dealing with. . . . How can I tell them to take care of themselves, and then they see me not taking care of myself? The problem is when to stop and recognize that you have reached your limit. You have to recognize that your own needs are part of the system you are dealing with as a therapist."[4]

How we decide to understand our experience is basically a *spiritual* question. One of the greatest and most exciting spiritual ideas of this moment in our culture is the renewed conviction that things fit together. The "basics," in other words, are not the pieces out of which something is made. The basics are the *interrelatedness* of all the pieces. That is where one must begin, including with the pieces of one's own life.

- What has your experience during the past year taught you about life?
- At this time of your life, what do you most value?
- What inspires you? What consoles you?
- How do you express your creativity?
- What makes you happy?

4. Quoted in Capra, *Uncommon Wisdom*, p. 281.

jottings

9

To Be Continued

Being your own authority about your life is not easy in today's world. Hopeful people have days when they feel hopeless and overwhelmed. Our mail boxes spawn an endless stream of letters, newspapers, periodicals, magazines, journals, and junk mail—all of it supposedly important if we are to stay in touch and be informed. To accelerate the gathering and dispensing of information, we have TV, radio, telephones, cellular phones, answering machines, computer e-mail and fax machines. It is difficult to live in the here and now when everything seems to be happening at once, and when much of what is happening is oppressive and depressing.

A sense of urgency adds still more pressure to the information overload that engulfs us. Being part of a family, raising a family, being part of a community, being present to those who need us and those whom we need—such pressures have always been with us and are not new or modern. But contemporary life adds many more stresses. The global community is in our living rooms, and our private space is not private anymore. Our sense of responsibility has been enlarged to include the condition of the whole planet and even outer space. It is one thing to have our awareness raised and expanded. It is another thing to become so overwhelmed that we feel hopeless, with no sense of authority over our own lives.

To get out from under this burden of hopelessness, many of us read another book or attend another seminar. We are surrounded by mentors and materials that facilitate insights. Books and workshops and seminars are useful tools. Admirable people inspire us. Even the busiest people, if only for reasons of health, force themselves to make time for exercise and take time out for spiritual pit-stops.

But relief for the feeling of hopelessness is not to be found *outside* ourselves. Sometimes we lose touch with humor, hope, joy, tenderness, compassion, generosity and forgiveness, while we search for our ideal self or the ideal community.

It is tempting to think that a good read makes us good persons. Purchasing ideas in order to feel good about oneself can be just another brand of consumerism. Often the insinuated promise of books and seminars, and the hope of those reading and participating, is trouble-free transformation. The myth of the good life encourages us to presume that we should never have to struggle, to do without or to be unhappy. Happiness is not a destination; it is a way of traveling.

Discernment is what we have to get down to after we have purchased the information, made some connections, and arrived at some insights. Discernment means sorting out our ideas and making critical judgments about our insights. Is the insight something that can be integrated into my life? Or is it just a wishful attempt to trade my story for another story, substitute my symbols with other symbols, or replace my rituals with other rituals?

Whatever we do—or leave undone—affects not only our own lives but those of many others. We need to be connected with other people, and we need to be involved in something that gives us a sense of purpose and commitment. Today many people are crossing traditional religious and social boundaries in their search for a community where they can be of service and make a contribution. And where they can celebrate.

To whom are you faithful? What groups or communities claim your loyalty?

Thus after discernment comes *application*. This means deciding to make changes. The quest for more spirit is translated into practice, and we *do* something.